Damascus

Damascus

Taste of a City

by
Marie Fadel

as told to
Rafik Schami

Translated by
Debra S Marmor and Herbert A Danner

HAUS PUBLISHING
London

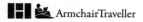 ArmchairTraveller

First published in German
© 2002 Sanssouci im Carl Hanser Verlag München Wien

First published in Great Britain in 2005
This English translation published in Great Britain in 2010 by
Haus Publishing Limited
70 Cadogan Place, London SW1X 9AH

English translation © Debra S. Marmor and Herbert A. Danner, 2005
English translation of additional material for revised edition © Peter Lewis, 2010

The moral right of the authors has been asserted

A CIP catalogue record for this book
is available from the British Library

ISBN 978-1-90659-883-9

Cover illustrations courtesy of Alamy Images. All photographs inside the book are courtesy of
Claudia Baumhöfer and Rafik Schami.
Map courtesy of Achim Norweg

Typset in Garamond by MacGuru Ltd
info@macguru.org.uk

Printed and bound in the UK by CPI Mackays, Chatham ME5 8TD

A CIP catalogue for this book is available from the British Library

Contents

To Damascus, years are only moments, decades are only flitting trifles of time. She measures time, not by days and months and years, but by the empires she has seen rise, and prosper and crumble to ruin. She is a type of immortality.

Mark Twain, *Innocents Abroad*

The Walking Tour, or
On the flavours and secrets of a city

I am often asked what I like doing most when I am not either telling stories or writing or reading. Every time I answer without having to think about it, cooking. Cooking for my wife, my son, my guests. Journalists are used to hearing authors respond, music or sport. But cooking is closely related to music and movement.

My mother was an excellent cook, a hostess and a connoisseur, but she is not the only source of my fondness for cooking. For that, you must travel much further back. Although I am a Christian, it is the Arab world and Islam that have shaped me, and, after a thorough study of the writings of Jesus and Muhammad, I can say: compared to that revolutionary ascetic Jesus, Muhammad was a great expert in matters of cooking and taste. You could fill a little book with his remarks on the subject – which would teach all those deluded, pleasure-hating Islamists a lesson.

This deeply rooted tradition of appreciating food taught me the difference between the necessity of filling a hungry stomach and the possibility of enjoyment.

Another source of my fondness for cooking is the greedy pleasure of the friends I entertain around my table. It's also true that, when I've spent days on a lecture tour, or sat at my writing desk, or taken part in political discussions, I need to relax by doing something at once physical and practical. Cooking has always helped me regain my lost sense of calm, put my thoughts in order and free my head of accumulated rubbish.

1

A cook has to live in the real world. For me, after a long stretch of writing, when I have lived day and night in the world of words, this becomes an essential challenge.

But that is not all that makes cooking so fascinating, and so closely related to writing. There is a comparable tension between the neutral starting materials (paper and ink in the case of one; raw meat, vegetables or fish in the case of the other) and the dream of the final product that can transport a gourmet into ecstasy.

The challenge is great and you may fail at any moment. Granted, in writing, as in cooking, professionalism gives you a certain confidence, but a cook who only follows proven steps, repeated hundreds of times, is at best worthy of a works canteen or college dining hall.

If it is truly to become an art, cooking must be as much of a risky experiment as writing. A word or a pinch of cayenne pepper too much, and the whole creation is a failure.

Perhaps this kinship between the two activities explains why I do not find it difficult to go back and forth between writing and cooking.

As some of the guests I entertain at my table work in publishing, I have often been asked why I don't write a cookbook. I have to laugh: there are so many projects that I thought up when I was sixteen, which I still haven't even made a start on.

No, there was no way I could free up two years to try out all the dishes and assemble the recipes. Of course, I said to myself, you would end up with an attractive and useful book. As the years passed, I even came to see how such a book should look: it would take you on a stroll through the Old City of Damascus, stopping along the way to visit family and friends and learn those secret recipes, tips and tricks that a stranger in a restaurant would never discover.

The idea had not yet fully matured when I began to think about how many different cultures have lived – and still do live – alongside and among each other in Damascus. That is the first secret of this ancient city. The people who have lived there have shaped its appearance, but its colours only truly unfold for the eyes of an expert. Visitors to Damascus recognise that special friendliness towards strangers which has always been one of the city's distinguishing features, but the origins of this openness generally remain hidden from them.

Building a book around a culinary-cultural walk through the city intrigued me, but there were two seemingly insurmountable barriers – time and geography. On the one hand all my other commitments and projects did not allow me the time. And on the other, how was I, living in exile, to visit family and friends in Damascus?

'No problem,' my sister Marie said on the telephone when I explained her the idea and the problem. 'We can walk through the city together on the phone. I'll visit the people and get them to cook me their favourite dishes. Our family here in Damascus can try out the recipes afterwards and I'll write them down together with all the secret tricks. I'll describe the places, alleyways, houses, personalities, curiosities and pearls of our Old City. It'll be a unique walk through the Old City. All you need to do is write down what I tell you. I'll send you the recipes to slot into the appropriate points in the text. You should try out the recipes again just to be certain. So I'll be your eyes in Damascus and you'll be my translator and taster in Germany. What do you say?' And she burst into laughter.

I was speechless.

Week after week, since then, I have gone for walks with my sister Marie – she on the telephone in Damascus and I on the telephone in Germany. We travelled the familiar alleys of the Old City, pausing at a memory, a house, a hammam (public bath), a gate or a shop, meeting relatives, visiting neighbours and friends. Marie talked and I saw, recreated by her voice, the streets, alleys, houses and kitchens. I tasted the spiciness of the dishes through her words and we listened and chuckled together at the often rhyming words of the street vendors, selling their goods, singing or offering up hymns of praise.

When you are considering a city with a great many attractions, naturally you have to make choices. Every book about Damascus focuses its greatest attention on the area around the Umayyad Mosque, but this book is different. In this one, the old Christian Quarter gets the most attention, and not just because the author is at home there and her relatives and friends live there,

3

but also because it is the most beautiful and colourful part of the city. Many books give it no more than half a page. In this respect, the book you have in your hands offers a totally new, little known picture of the city of Damascus.

My joy came not only from strolling through the city, but also from realising how the diversity of peoples that have migrated through Damascus have combined to create an outstanding cuisine.

Marie would return home from our jaunts, cook everything and write down the recipes and their peculiarities. I transcribed the walks from the tape recorder that captured every telephone conversation. I have only added things where I felt that an outsider would have difficulty understanding some particular detail.

We wandered through Damascus for a year. She in the city and I – almost torn apart by longing – on the telephone in Germany. There is no city in the world I love as much as Damascus. It is said: 'When a man has lived seven years in Damascus, Damascus lives in him.' I lived in Damascus for 25 years.

Marie tested all the recipes she gathered. After consulting with me, she calculated all the quantities for four to six people, although usually in Damascus you would prepare two to three times that quantity. No book can absolutely determine cooking times: no variety of rice or bean or cut of meat is exactly the same as another. No oven, gas flame or frying pan is so standard that you can always depend on the same temperature. You need to be bold and curious: slavish cooking-by-numbers this is not. My second sister, Thérése, and my sister-in-law, Atir, assisted Marie. No matter how simple it may seem, you cannot cook Damascene food half-heartedly. You have to put your whole soul into it – preferably in the company of friends.

In the autumn of 2001, my publishing friends Felicitas Feilhauer and Claudia Baumhöver visited my family in Damascus and brought back not only many photographs, but also the handwritten Arabic originals of the recipes – impressive evidence of the great art of cooking in Damascus. The rest was easy. The pleasures of my new profession as taster were my best reward.

Rafik Schami

'The green gardens surround Damascus as the aura does the moon.'

Ibn Jubair, Andalucian traveller, ca 1184

Joy, or
On saints, twisting alleyways and good-tempered salads

The Old City has seven gates, which is exactly how many years you have to live there to understand it. Damascus is the oldest city in the world to have been inhabited continuously up to the present day. The longer a stranger stays there, the more his first, immediate fascination gives way to a deep love for the filigreed forms of this lively metropolis.

The Prophet Muhammad is said to have refused to enter Damascus. Approaching from the south, he reached a suburb now called Kadam, which means 'foot' in Arabic, in order to emphasise the holiness of a place touched by the Prophet's foot. Muhammad saw the city with its gardens from Kadam and said, more or less, that man may only enter paradise once. He chose the one hereafter.

Naturally there are good and very good restaurants to be found in Damascus, some with beautiful, dream-like gardens or a tranquil historic location, others modern and perfectly organised. But no amount of elaborately manufactured atmosphere can match up to the secret corners of an old Damascene kitchen.

So many peoples and cultures have passed through Damascus. They have left their mark on the language, on the buildings and in the soul of the inhabitants. Damascene cooking is a living witness and delicious memorial to this many-sided history.

We are standing at the head of a very famous and ancient street, running from East to West, called simply Straight Street. This street, already called Straight Street by Luke in the Acts of the Apostles, defined the cityscape at the time of Paul and continues to shape the Old City to this day. It was once 26 metres wide, but over the centuries its capable merchants and craftsmen have expanded ever further into the street. Today there are spots where the street is not even 10 metres across. Every morning, when I see how a merchant sets out his stacks of wooden boxes or crates of vegetables, fruit or pistachios on the pavement or even the road itself, stretching his shop deep into the street, I always have to laugh at how discreet he is in taking over the area in front of his shop, and yet how obvious it is that, for several hundred thousand such mornings, every shopkeeper and craftsman along this street has done the same trick.

Damascus still today bears the marks of the Greeks who originally laid it out. The Old City is based on the classical design of the Ancient Greek town planner Hippodamus of Miletus, but with the added, magical charm of its unmistakable oval shape. Many have compared it, rightly, to a paper kite, of the sort that children have.

It was through the Eastern Gate, *Bab ash-Sharqi* in Arabic, that in 635AD the Arabs stormed what was then one of the most beautiful cities in the world and then, as they stood within its walls, fell in love. The warriors, plagued by thirst since their childhoods in the desert, had found paradise on earth: a city of gardens and, most importantly, plentiful, clean water. Damascus became the capital of their global empire for almost 90 years. The Arabs tolerated the resident Christian and Jewish minorities – most of whom earned a living as skilful craftsmen – for pragmatic reasons. Being desert nomads, the Arabs had no particular fondness for handicrafts and, since they wished to build the country into a mighty empire rather than just plunder it, they needed these knowledgeable craftsmen. Though the Arabs declined to expel them, the Christians and Jews had to pay a hefty poll tax, yet they saw the Arabic Muslims as their liberators from the hated Romans, a feeling only strengthened by their mild treatment at the hands of their conquerors. So the Muslims tolerated the

8

religious minorities – with certain limits on their political rights – and allowed them to remain, while they in turn did not try to flee but instead soon became an essential element of the Arabic culture.

Damascus has a similar relationship to its minorities to the present day. In no other city have members of all cultures and religions survived fifteen centuries of turbulent history. The city and its calming climate have certainly got something to do with it. People often speak, not with envy, of the exceptional charm and prudence of the Damascene character. The first caliph of the Umayyad, Mu'awiyah, said: 'When my whip can do the job, I do not draw my sword and when my tongue suffices, I do not use either.' He most likely learned that from the Damascenes. He was governor of the metropolis for many years before elevating himself to caliph and founder of a dynasty. His wife, the mother of his successor on the throne, was a Christian; his court poet al Akhtal was a Christian; as was his finance minister, Mansur Bin Sergun. The latter's son would later become a world-famous Christian saint, the lyricist and theologian John of Damascus.

But back to Straight Street. The area near the Eastern Gate has many pretty spots. If you graciously overlook the horrible signs encouraging tourists to purchase their oriental souvenirs, you can enjoy the quiet of the modest alleys and beautifully maintained houses. Here and there, even in the Old City, you can see the dreadful effects of modernity, with its ugly concrete and rusted iron, but most of the Old City has been well protected. Next to businesses selling groceries and household appliances you will find unusual tradesmen, most often in tiny shops. For example, there is a hair salon that looks fairly medieval from the outside but houses a stylist of international calibre. A few steps farther on you encounter a man who stands bent over a carpet hour upon hour. Silently and humbly that man practices one of the highest arts – the repair and restoration of old carpets with complicated patterns – an art far more difficult than weaving the original carpet.

At home once, when a spark flew out of the wood-burning stove and burned a plate sized hole in a Persian carpet, our mother thought our father would have a heart attack as soon as he saw the damage. All his life our father preferred to sit on the floor and of every object in the house, this carpet was his favourite. But when our mother showed him the black hole, he nodded and said: 'Thank God you discovered the fire in time. Ali will fix the carpet.' Ali took one week. When his errand boy brought the carpet back, it was no longer possible to detect the damaged spot.

Carpet restorers work with wool threads that have to be more or less as old as the damaged carpet itself. They buy newly dyed wool threads every year and lay them out to go through the same climatically induced changes as would those in a carpet.

If you now turn right into the first alley after the Eastern Gate, you are standing right on the coordinates of an historical event that probably only could have happened in Damascus. It was here that Saul became Paul. The historic chapel dedicated to the man who, according to legend, healed Saul's blindness during his 'Damascus experience' is located here. The man's name was Ananias, and the alley is named for him. As a Christian convert, Paul now had to hide from his henchmen and flee in the night through the Abbara, our alley, and over the wall at its end. A chapel now stands at the spot where Paul was lowered down the wall in a basket. We will come back to that later when we go down our alley.

Back to Hanania Alley. Aunt Salime, a distant cousin of my mother's, lives not far from the subterranean Chapel of Ananias. If someone were to ask me whether there are people who really understand how to live, I would not hesitate to suggest Aunt Salime and Uncle Farid. Perhaps it is a coincidence – and then again, maybe it is not – that our walk should begin with Aunt Salime, a mistress of the art of living, and end with Uncle Farid, one of the greatest hosts on earth, who lives far away in the Qaimariyya quarter near the Umayyad Mosque. He is the greatest fire-work of a host in all of Damascus; Aunt Salime is cheerfulness incarnate. Uncle Farid is a strong character, but his life has been easy with such a wife at his side, a woman whom he has idolised since childhood and who worships him to this day after 40 years of marriage.

Aunt Salime, in contrast, has only ever had bad luck. But hearing her laugh, one would think she'd stepped out of fortune's fountain. The reality is quite different: first her husband disappeared off to Canada with her best friend just one year after they married, leaving her behind in Damascus, the scene of her mortification. Then her house burned down, all the way to its foundations. She was at the cinema with a friend when the fire broke out. 'Imagine how lucky I am,' she said to me a day after the disaster. 'The head fireman said I wouldn't have stood a chance of survival if I'd been at home. God be thanked that Alia invited me to the cinema. The film was good.' And she laughed.

My mother always referred to Aunt Salime as un-sinkable. It was not just that she always rose again. It was her magical laughter that infected all of us and made her one of the most popular people in the quarter.

Aunt Salime invites a few women to her home almost every Sunday, especially in the spring and summer, and together they prepare that most famous of all Damascene salads – tabbouleh. In any given year I have been to her Sunday gatherings at least five or six times. It is always a feast for the palate, eyes, ears, laughter muscles and heart. Aunt Salime is the conductor, while we chop, crush and mix. She brings everything together into one mighty salad and then we sit for hours at her table, eating, laughing and talking.

Aunt Salime thinks tabbouleh is the only salad that is never served on sad occasions. Perhaps this is because of its bright colours and flavourful herbs, which are not considered appropriate for mourning. You may laugh at my aunt's words, but in all my fifty years, I have never yet experienced a family in mourning preparing tabbouleh for themselves or their guests.

Tabbouleh is a parsley salad. Everything else is just an ingredient. In this salad, parsley is used not as a herb but as the main element.

❊ تبولة ❊

Tabbouleh
Parsley Salad

400 g finely ground burghul (cracked wheat)
2 large bunches of flat-leafed parsley (ca. 600 g)
1 kg vine tomatoes
2 red and 2 green sweet peppers
1 cucumber
4 carrots
1 bunch spring onions
1 bunch radishes
2 cloves of garlic
4 small or 2 large lemons
1 tbsp dried mint (best would be the slightly bitter variety from
   the Mediterranean, called Na'na'. In the summer, it tastes
   even better to use 1 bunch of fresh mint, and add 1 bunch
   fresh basil and a handful of fresh thyme leaves.)
Salt and pepper
250ml (yes, that much!) olive oil

Wash the burghul, cover with cold water and let it soak for 15
minutes.

Remove stalks and stems from the parsley and finely chop with
a knife.

Wash, prepare and finely dice the vegetables and then put them
in a large salad bowl with the parsley. Peel and crush the garlic
cloves, adding to the bowl. Add the lemon juice and burghul.
Add the mint, salt and pepper and mix thoroughly. Then pour
the olive oil over it and stir it in.

Allow the salad to stand for 10 minutes and then thoroughly
mix once more.

❊ Burghul can be stored for a long time, if you keep it well sealed in cloth bags and in a dry place. Burghul can 'breathe' in cloth bags, as Aunt Salime puts it.

Aunt Salime always serves the Tabbouleh salad in round bowls, lined with fresh lettuce leaves.

The salad is wonderfully filling, and can be served with any kind of drink.

Tabbouleh only tastes good when it is fresh.

The joy of life or
Of streets smelling of musk
and 'our daily bread'

If you return to Straight Street from Hanania Alley, you will discover the little Armenian Alley on the opposite side, on which stands the Armenian Orthodox Church. The Armenians are an Indo-Germanic people, whose history has been quite tragic. They have had the bad luck that their country, like Kurdistan, has rival imperial powers as its close neighbours: the Russians, the Persians, the Arabs and the Ottomans (later the Turks) have all stood in the way of Armenian independence. Thousands fled because of war, persecution and barbaric pogroms (particularly in 1895/96 and 1914/15), and many sought a safe haven in Syria. Armenians have always preferred to live in cities.

They speak their own language, which – unlike the typical Arabic writing – is written from left to right in a characteristic Armenian script. They live in a close-knit community and rarely marry outside of it. Armenians are particularly well-known for three things: their diligence, their fondness for anything to do with technology, and, last but not least, excellent air-dried lean beef in a spicy coating. They call it Pasturma – a delicacy whose quality has lately fallen victim to mass production. If the Pasturma is stringy and moist, and the wrapping is a floury spicy mush, do not go near it.

The taste of Pasturma also depends on how thinly it is sliced. The best bet is to purchase it from a grocer who understands just how wafer thin it needs to be cut. It is better to take chunks than whole slices that have been sliced thickly. Father always said: 'Pasturma only tastes right if you can see the light through the thin slices.'

But back to Straight Street. Another few steps and Dsha'far Alley, which more or less runs parallel to Hanania Alley, is on the right.

At the end, Dsha'far Alley leads into Masbaq Alley, where our brother Mtanios lives with his wife and three sons. Mtanios loves to laugh and bakes outstanding S'fiha and Mnaquish bi Zahtar. Apart from that, he (like many Arab men) is totally useless in the kitchen. We'll come back to the lovely S'fiha when we reach our bakery in Bab Touma. These days, for convenience, you are more likely to buy S'fiha from a bakery, but Mtanios is convinced that it is still better from his own kitchen.

On the left a few metres from Dsha'far Alley you can see the beautiful portal of the Syrian Catholic Church, one of the oldest churches in Damascus. Another few steps along Straight Street, about level with the Syrian Catholic Church, and you come to the entrance to al Kasbah Alley on the right, now called al Ouqaibeh Alley. What a funny name! Hardly anyone knows what al Ouqaibeh means. The name of the alley will always be al Kasbah to me. This alley leads to the old city wall and to the entire Christian quarter. Misq Alley opens on the left directly at the top of this alley. What a lovely name for a tiny alley – *misq* means musk in Arabic. I can only hope no bureaucrat in the city administration gets so bored that he has the bright idea of giving it a new name as well. Misq Alley branches out and develops into a little labyrinth of calm. If you keep to the left, though, you will easily find your way out again onto the broad street that leads to Bab Touma.

My school friend Alia lives in the middle of Misq Alley. Alia fell ill with cancer at the age of ten and the doctors gave her less than a year to live. But she fought with an iron will; and, though pale and bent, she has survived her illness and her three doctors. She has stayed single and does not live badly on her inheritance. Every time I allude to her ordeal she laughs and says: 'I already knew as a young girl that life was wonderful, and didn't want the angel of death to take me before I had tasted it'.

'And have you had enough now?' I joked once.

'Are you kidding? I'm only on the starter,' she retorted and spluttered with laughter.

I visit her at least once a month, and, on the rare occasions that I announce myself ahead of time by telephone, there are guaranteed to be stuffed pasties. Alia knows I particularly like to eat her pasties.

An absolute prerequisite for all varieties of pasties is good dough. Of course you can make pasties and rolls with any kind of dough and stuffing, but to make Alia's delicacies it is best to stick to the recipe for bread dough.

۞ فطائر عجين ۞
Pasties à la Alia

The Bread Dough
1 kg wholemeal flour (preferably 50% wheat, 50% rye)
20 g salt
ca. ½ litre water
20 g fresh yeast
3 tbsp oil (preferably sunflower oil)

If necessary, sift the flour together with the salt. Mix in the cold water and knead. Break up the yeast in a bowl and dissolve in about 50 ml lukewarm water. Add to the dough and continue to knead until the dough is soft and firm. Add the oil and again knead through thoroughly. Turn the dough out on a lightly floured work surface and knead. Frequently stretch the dough lengthwise using the heel of your hand and then fold it over on itself. Repeat the process until the dough is smooth, supple and elastic. Place the dough in an oiled bowl, cover with a clean tea towel. Set in a warm place and leave to rise until doubled in size. When you come to work the dough further, thoroughly knead through again on a marble or wooden board that has been lightly dusted with flour.

Bread is the Arabs' basic foodstuff, no matter where they live. In Syria, as in most Arab states, it is subsidized by the state. Its price is a political issue and it is not unusual for an increase in the price of bread to cause unrest: in Egypt it once led to a massive public uprising. In many places bread is called life, Arabic Aisch, or blessing, Arabic Ni'ma, and there is nothing an Arab will pick up off the floor with greater reverence than a piece of bread.

Only a Middle Easterner could have written the 'Lord's Prayer'. After the supplicant reassures God 'hallowed be Thy name, Thy kingdom come, Thy will be done, on earth as it is in heaven,' the very first thing he demands is 'Give us this day our daily bread.' We don't want our daily meat, vegetables or milk, but our daily bread. And the word 'daily' is meant in all seriousness here. The Damascenes prefer to eat their bread fresh from the oven. Hardly anyone buys yesterday's bread, even at half price.

Today's classic Arabic bread looks just the same today as it did two thousand years ago. It is, by the way, the gift of the Middle East to the Italians. The Romans discovered the pocket or flat bread, pitta, in the Near East. Its shape fascinated the soldiers. In a hot oven, the thin shape of dough at first puffs itself up into a balloon and then later collapses as the steam escapes, leaving two equal discs of dough that are crispy on the outside and soft on the inside. You can easily slit it open and fill the resulting pocket (but don't overfill it) with whatever filling you like – sweet, savoury, sour, vegetarian, meat, egg, and so on – transforming the bread into a handy sandwich. The bread and its contents can then be rolled up into a nice roll, which the Damascenes affectionately call a 'bride'.

Two thousand years ago the Roman soldiers took the pitta with them to Italy. Their beloved focaccia bread later developed from the pitta, and in Sicily, it became the famous pizza.

These days every Turkish or Arab grocer stocks Arab flat bread. But if you still want to make it yourself, here are the necessary steps:

17

Form 8 to 12 balls of equal size from about 1 kg of bread dough, freshly prepared following the method described above but which has not yet risen. Cover with a clean cloth and allow to rise for 20 minutes.

Preheat oven to highest heat (regular oven or fan assisted).

On a lightly floured work surface, dust the dough balls with flour and roll out into discs about 2.5 mm thick and 20 cm in diameter.

Place the discs on a lightly floured baking sheet, ensuring they do not touch each other. Cover with a clean, dry cloth and allow to prove for half an hour.

Pasties with various fillings

Of course you can choose to serve only one filling for a meal, but it is better for the eyes and palate to prepare a variety of fillings and to divide up the dough. You can of course try out your own fillings. Here we present two classics that Alia always serves: Pasties With Meat and Pasties With Spinach.

❉ We usually serve a colourful salad with these pasties. In Damascus, some hosts serve small bowls of natural yoghurt as an accompaniment to pasties with meat. You put a few spoonfuls of it on your plate and dip pieces of the pasties in it. But Alia does not like yoghurt, so she always serves her pasties with a salad instead. Her pasties are so small that you do not need any cutlery. After the salad course, you pick which pasties you want from the large serving bowls, put them on your own plate and then eat them with your fingers.

Meat filling

As always, the quantities are for 4–6 people and the filling is based on dough that has been prepared from 1 kg flour. Of course the quantities should be reduced if you are making other fillings as well.

3 tbsp sunflower oil or butterfat
3 onions
750 g lean beef mince
50 g pine nuts
1 garlic clove
1 tsp thyme
1 tsp salt
1 tsp pepper
1 tsp cinnamon

Preheat a metal frying pan, adding enough oil or butterfat to lightly coat the bottom. Peel and finely chop the onions and sauté in the pan until golden. Add the meat and brown. In a second, smaller pan slightly brown the pine nuts (careful not to burn them) and add to the meat. Peel and crush the garlic clove, adding it to the meat. Allow the mixture to fry for 10 minutes over a medium heat, stirring frequently and breaking the mince up into smaller pieces. Season the mince mixture to taste; remove from heat; and allow to cool.

Spinach Stuffing
1 kg fresh spinach
4 onions
2 tsp salt
2 large garlic cloves
1 tsp pepper
2 tsp freshly ground coriander seeds
2 tbsp sumac
Freshly ground nutmeg
1 lemon
100 ml olive oil
5 walnuts

Sumac is an edible fruit of the stag's horn sumac genus that grows in the Mediterranean regions. The tart fruity powder can be purchased at Arabic and Turkish grocers. We will return to it in our chapter on spices (al-Bzouriyya).

Wash the spinach thoroughly and remove stalks and stems. Using your hands, squeeze out the water and finely chop the spinach. Sprinkle with a bit of salt and allow to draw for 10 minutes. Peel the onions and chop finely. Mix the spinach with the onions, add crushed garlic, salt pepper, coriander, sumac, nutmeg, lemon juice and olive oil, and mix thoroughly. Peel and chop the walnuts and add to the spinach. Mix thoroughly again.

The filling is placed on the prepared dough discs. Draw up the dough around the filling and press the edges together. The pasties can be formed into any shape. The only important thing is that the dough is well sealed.

Place the finished pasties on a greased baking sheet and lightly brush their surface with sunflower oil.

Bake for 12–15 minutes in an oven preheated to ca. 200° C/400° F/Gas Mark 6. At the end, put under the grill for 2–3 minutes to crisp the pasties until they are golden brown.

The hurdler, or
Of patriarchs and olives

When you return to Straight Street from Misq Alley and then continue westward, you pass the little Arisha Mosque on the left. The broad al-Saitun Alley opens almost immediately beyond that on the left. This is where the school is. It used to be called the Patriarchal School and was one of three Christian elite schools. This is the school you attended before you emigrated to Germany. It has now been nationalised and has the boring name *Inaja*, which has all manner of Arabic meanings including trouble, torment, effort and divine providence.

The Patriarch of the Eastern Catholic Church has his head office in this alley. And until recently, my friend Widad lived at the beginning of it.

Widad had a tragic fate. Her parents wanted to marry her to her cousin. But she loved a good-looking boy from the neighbourhood. He was the heartthrob of all the women. When her parents found out about Widad's love, they tried everything to get their daughter to see reason. But Widad loved only this one boy and was willing on his account to suffer as many agonies as her parents could dream up. In those days, strictness and inflexibility were nothing unusual in Arab society. All Arab literature thrives on tragedies of thwarted love.

Widad bore her parents' hardheartedness with the patience of a fanatic waiting for her moment. For her it was like a great challenge: she wanted to overcome a society that forbade such a love. Then one night it was all too much. The young man resolved to undergo the dangerous adventure and fled with her.

Her mother's cries echoed through the alleys and were repeated in the mouths of gossips until every last person in the village knew that Widad had been 'kidnapped'. That was the hypocritical code word for a daughter who had eloped. The term 'kidnapped' not only relieves the parents of any responsibility but also announces that as soon as the 'kidnapper' is caught, the liaison will be ended on the spot. In some areas a death sentence is pronounced on the renegade couple.

Widad, knowing she would not survive the reunion if her father found her, hid. For four years she lived with her lover in secret in Aleppo. For a long time her parents thundered, but when they found out she had brought a beautiful baby daughter into the world, they allowed the priest to persuade them to a reconciliation.

Widad's happiness, or at least what she naively thought was her happiness, lasted another three years. In their seventh year, she discovered her husband had not one, not two, but an entire flock of lovers, and he was the leader of the flock. The bitter ending was still to come. Before she could confront him, the faithless wretch disappeared overseas with one of his lovers and was never seen again. It was thought that he was in Italy, Mexico or the United States.

As the old story goes, when a snake is injured, it bites the wound to prevent ants being attracted to it and eating their way into the body through the wound until the snake is nothing but an empty shell. Relatives are ants. But Widad clenched her teeth, suffered her defeat in silence and worked hard to support her daughter and herself. Her good parents helped her so she would not slide into poverty. But no parent can heal heartbreak.

Though men swarmed around her, Widad lived only for her daughter. She worked as a cook in a good restaurant. Today her daughter Haiat, the source of all Widad's pride, studies architecture. And if you were not familiar with Widad's tragic past, you would think she had lived a life blessed with good fortune. In reality, however, every day has been a battle for as long as she can remember. But Widad is one of those people who face her challenges with laughter.

When it comes to cooking, she is a master of improvisation. If there were a prize for successful use of leftovers, she would be the winner. Poverty was her teacher.

Her tastiest dish is a salad, a salad which is actually also an elegant way to make old bread appetising.

Fattoush
Bread Salad

The firmer and fresher the vegetables used in this salad, the better it will taste. In Damascus the leftover bread pieces are toasted before use. The Damascene flat breads are wafer thin and after toasting resemble the crisp breads (rye or sesame) widely available in Europe.

500 g cucumber
500 g red and green sweet peppers
1 kg tomatoes
1 bunch radishes
200 g lamb's lettuce
1 bunch shallots or 2 large onions
1 large bunch parsley
1 small bunch mint
a few basil leaves
200 g pitted black olives
200 g pitted green olives
1 garlic clove
3 tbsp vinegar
150 ml olive oil
Salt and pepper
250 g crisp bread

Thoroughly clean the vegetables and lettuce. Cut the cucumbers, peppers, tomatoes, radishes and peeled shallots (or onions) into small dice and place in a large bowl. Remove roots and wilted leaves from the lettuce and add the rest to vegetable mixture. Wash and finely chop the parsley, mint and basil leaves; add to the salad. Add the olives. Crush the garlic into a bowl and mix together with the vinegar, oil, salt and pepper. Add to the salad and mix thoroughly.

Break the crisp bread into small pieces and mix into the salad just before serving.

❋ *If fresh mint is not available, then 1 tsp of dried mint will work as well.*

At the end of al-Saitun Alley is the seat of the Patriarch and on the left is the school. Just on the right you come to a shady cul-de-sac that ends in front of your friend Joseph's house. This massive house has two doors. One of them is here, practically in front of the school. The other is in our alley, right across from our front door. In the old days, as was customary everywhere, the doors were open.

How often you and your brother and many other boys in our alley angered the residents of the house, cutting through their house on your way to school early in the morning, late as always, taking the shortcut through their house, almost blind with excitement, whipping in through the door in our alley, across the courtyard and then out the other side onto al-Saitun Alley – all to save the seven minutes it would have taken to go the horseshoe-shaped long way around! Seven minutes made the difference between a feeling of self-satisfaction and disaster, usually involving extra homework as punishment for your lateness.

Back to al-Saitun Alley. A lonely widower lives at the little shady end of the cul-de-sac. He is my schoolmate Nadshla's father. Whether out of prophetic foresight or empty chance, his parents named him Halim (the patient one).

He was orphaned at a young age because the Druse uprising against the French occupiers took place then. His parents were Christians and lived in As Suwayda, a city far to the south, which was the insurgents' stronghold. The French bombed it and Halim's parent died in the wreckage of their house. He had been playing somewhere outside and thus escaped death. He grew up, became an apprentice to an auto mechanic and finally married a woman from the neighbourhood. She gave him four children, three boys and a girl – my girlfriend Nadshla. Halim doted on his wife and spoiled her in any way he possibly could. And it seemed that life was smiling on him. But suddenly, the heavens again darkened. Two Arab dictators saw the Druse minority as a threat, even though they had been the only ones who had led an uprising worth mentioning against the French occupation. The bloody tyrant Adib Shishakli became the first Arab ruler to bomb his own people when he bombed the Druse territories in the winter of 1953–54. Shrapnel hit Halim's wife in the head. She died immediately.

Halim left As Suwayda, his beloved city, because he could no longer live there with the memories of his wife and parents. He sought out far distant Damascus to make a new start and to forget. To his great fortune, he quickly found a decent partner, with whom he started up a garage. It generated enough income to provide a good life for his children and an old cousin of his became housekeeper and governess to the children.

The cousin was a nice lady who lovingly cared for the children, but she was not much of a cook. On Sundays, when Halim had the day off, he started cooking for his children and the cousin himself. And because it is customary for Damascene Christians to eat Kibbeh on Sundays, he kept cooking different variants of this noble dish for his children on Sundays. He cooked vast quantities so there was always plenty to eat for everyone. From then on, the children only wanted to eat Kibbeh on Sundays.

Then, as though there had not been enough death in Halim's life, he lost all three of his sons, one after the other, as they died in the many wars that plagued the Middle East. Halim seemed to be at the end. But man is a worker of miracles. This man, who is now past 70, survived, returned to his garage and continued to work. At first his daughter Nadshla, my girlfriend, only wanted to live for him. But he begged her to follow her own path and to give him a grandchild. Nadshla married her childhood sweetheart, a sly fox of a hairdresser, with whom she still lives and who gave her three children – all of whom are spitting images of their grandfather.

Two years ago, Nadshla moved to Aleppo in the north. Her husband had inherited a large house. But Halim did not want to move again. He stayed in his house with the old cousin who now cared for him. Nadshla rings me every time she comes to Damascus because her father insists on inviting all her girlfriends, along with their children and husbands, to a farewell supper. And what does he serve? Kibbeh in every possible variation.

Kibbeh is also pronounced Kebbeh or Kubbeh. It is a wonderful dish made of lean meat and fine burghul (called Kibbeh Dough), which is shaped and stuffed, fried or baked and served in many different ways. This mild but delicious dish is counted among the special meals that are normally only eaten on Sundays or holidays.

Kibbeh

Kibbeh Dough
500 g lean beef shank meat
250 g finely ground burghul wheat
1 tsp allspice
1 tsp cinnamon
1 tsp pepper
1 tsp salt
1 pinch freshly grated nutmeg

In the old days, you used to have to use lots of elbow grease and a mortar and pestle to grind down the beef. Now it is done effortlessly with a food processor. Finely chop the meat twice (you can either ask your butcher to do this or do it yourself) and place it in the refrigerator.

Briefly wash the burghul, cover with water and allow to soak for 10 minutes.

Add meat, burghul and the finely ground spices in portions to the food processor and mix again until it comes together in a smooth Kibbeh Dough. If the dough is too crumbly or too firm and dry, add a few tbsp of cold water and knead it through. Chill the dough.

❀ *It is useful to have a bowl of cold water at hand when working with Kibbeh. It is easier to work the dough with wet hands.*

Always replace the dough in the refrigerator and avoid letting it get too warm. In this way the meat stay fresher and firmer during preparation.

Fried Slices of Kibbeh

Using damp hands, make small walnut sized balls from the Kibbeh dough and then press then flat between your hands to form a slice. Smooth the edge. Place the slices next to each other on a large baking sheet or tray. When the tray is full, cover it with foil (so the slices do not stick together) and place a second layer of slices on top. If several people are helping, you can start the frying at this point: professionals can shape the second layer at the same time as they fry the first, but for beginners it's better to do all the shaping first, to avoid too much of a rush while frying.

Put a generous amount of sunflower oil (at least 3 cm deep) in a deep pan. Heat the oil rapidly and then fry the slices over a medium heat so that they are cooked on the inside before they become crispy on the outside.

The Kibbeh slices can have a diameter of 15 cm, but should not be any thicker than 1 cm, or they will taste doughy.

The simplest form of Kibbeh is baked on a baking tray. A nobler variation is Kibbeh with stuffing. It is the filling that gives this dish its particular distinction.

The Stuffing

100 g butterfat
2 medium onions
500 g beef mince
50 g pine nuts
1 tbsp allspice
1 tsp salt
1 pinch of pepper

Heat the butterfat in a pan and sweat the onions in it until they are softened but not browned. Stir in the meat and brown for about 10 minutes, then allow to cool. In a second, smaller pan, fry the pine nuts in a bit of sunflower oil until golden and immediately take out of the pan, otherwise they will go dark brown and bitter. Add pine nuts, allspice, salt and pepper to the meat and thoroughly mix.

Baked Kibbeh from the Baking Tray

This is a delight for the eyes and palate. Most Damascene Christians eat this kind of Kibbeh – a cake made of two layers of Kibbeh with a spicy filling – on Sundays.

Generously grease a baking tray, preferably a round one made of steel or aluminium. Halve the Kibbeh dough. One half will form the bottom layer. In order to cover the tray without leaving any gaps, take a piece of the Kibbeh dough and press it into a flat slab between your wet hands. Lay it on the tray. Keep repeating this piece by piece until the entire tray is covered, slightly overlapping the slabs as you place them on the tray. Use your moistened hand to flatten the 'seams' to create a smooth flat surface. Make sure there are no gaps anywhere. Spread the filling evenly over the bottom layer. Now comes the difficult part: the top layer. Do the same as you did for the bottom layer, but try not to press too hard on the filling so it stays airy. Again make sure there are no gaps and none of the filling is visible.

Now run a flat knife around the edge so that the cake will lift easily from the tray later. This is important, because the cake will shrink a bit and if the edges are free to move there will be no tears in the cake. Preheat the oven to 200° C/400° F/ Gas Mark 6.

You can decorate the cake in a simple but attractive way, popular among Damascene cooks, by cutting a diamond pattern into the top layer with a sharp knife. First draw parallel lines across the entire surface of the cake, then turn the tray a little and again etch parallel lines across the surface. Take care to not disturb the Kibbeh dough or to cut through it.

Now distribute small knobs of butterfat (ca. 50 g) over the top of the cake. Bake 15–20 minutes in the preheated oven. If necessary, put under the grill for 2 minutes at the end to achieve a crisp surface.

Serve the kibbeh hot from the tray, by cutting triangular slices with their points in the centre, just like a cake. If the tray is square or rectangular, then serve square or rectangular pieces. Always use a sharp knife to remove the pieces so that all three layers end up on the plate.

This dish goes well with a colourful salad.

Dusty microcosm, or
How a little alley
made world history

If you now leave al-Saitun Alley, return to Straight Street and continue west, you come to several beautiful restored houses on the right. The most famous of these are the houses of the Kashisho and Shawi families, built near the end of the Ottoman period, which those two families have lovingly restored to their original glory.

The next alley after al-Saitun is our humble Abbara, where several splendid examples of Arab interior design hide behind inconspicuous clay walls. But that is not the most exciting aspect of this alley. Its name gives the clue: *abbara* means gateway. This is the alley I mentioned earlier, down which St Paul fled after his conversion. Only because his escape succeeded was he able to proclaim his new religion to the world. As a result, Abbara Alley has exerted a greater influence on mankind than several global empires put together. But the alley's residents don't much care: they just carry on with their everyday lives.

Our family has lived in this alley for over 60 years. You, too, spent your childhood and youth here, before you left for Germany. I know almost all the alleys and streets of Damascus, and I have rarely encountered as many unusual people as I have here. Do you remember we had a women's team for basketball and volleyball as early as 1963? And that, for five years from 1965, our alley was the only one in all of Damascus to post a newsletter on the wall?

Book upon book could be written about the Abbara; as far as I am aware, its residents already populate your books. Every day new events take place that you do not get to experience. I have just remembered one that happened only the other day.

The family of Adnan the taxi driver was given a lovely fruit basket as a gift. Adnan immediately thought of his brother, a tiler, who was somewhat poorer and lived a few houses along, so he gave the fruit basket to him. The next day Adnan's brother praised the amazing freshness of the fruit. But in truth he had not even touched it. He had a friend at the end of the alley who lived a very unhealthy lifestyle, a heavy smoker who ate almost exclusively cheap, fatty meat. The tiler gave the man the basket saying: 'A few vitamins will do you good. Perhaps you will get a bit of colour in your face.'

This bachelor seems to have had no idea what to do with the fruit, so he gave it to his neighbour, an old widow. She thought the gift was wonderful, but she pitied the taxi driver's children, who always seemed a bit pale, so she gave the basket to their mother saying: 'The children need the fresh fruit. It is already too late for me and I do not have any teeth anymore.'

And so the fruit basket found its way back to the taxi driver. He and his wife had to laugh out loud when they discovered that not only his brother, but also every single one of the recipients had complimented their respective gift giver on how wonderful the fruit tasted.

Families tend to live together in large houses in this alley. Life is lived openly. Whilst this public way of life can become tiresome, it encourages hospitality.

Even if I were not my mother's daughter, I would have still liked Hanne just for her humour, her hospitality and her lentil dishes. Do you remember the answer she gave every time we asked why she cooked such vast quantities? She claimed it was because she had the feeling someone would drop in on us unannounced. In truth, relatives were always stopping by without advance notice, as is the custom in Damascus. This never upset Mother. She just brought out clean plates for them and they ate with us, as a matter of course. After all, the bowls were full.

Like all mountain-dwellers, Mother liked lentils. They are very nutritious and taste marvellous, which is why they are called the 'poor man's meat'. The Bible tells us that Esau sold his birthright to his brother Jacob for a plate of lentils.

Mother cooked numerous varieties of lentil soup and all of them tasted good, but her masterpiece was always Damascus's most famous lentil dish: Mujadarra.

❋ مجدرة ❋

Mujadarra
Lentil, burghul and onion dish

This is the noblest way to prepare lentils. The dish is mentioned as a Damascene speciality as early as a cookbook from the 12th century. Farmers call Mujadarra the 'knee strengthener', to suggest the energy this dish provides.

Mujadarra is a simple, good value and tasty dish that again confirms my theory that flavour need not be dependent on price.

300 g brown unpeeled lentils
300 g coarsely ground burghul wheat
2 tsp salt
1 tsp pepper
1 pinch coriander
1 pinch cinnamon
250 ml olive oil
3 large onions
300 ml sunflower oil (for frying)

Wash the lentils and place in a saucepan. Cook in about 1.5 l water for 20 minutes. Then stir in the washed burghul, salt and spices. Add sufficient water to just cover. Bring to the boil briefly and then leave to cook over a low heat for 10 minutes. Turn off the heat and let stand covered for 5 minutes. Pour over the olive oil in a thin stream and leave it for another 5 minutes to absorb.

Mujadarra becomes a classic when combined with fried onions. Peel the onions and slice in rings. Heat the sunflower oil in a pan and fry the onions until crispy over medium heat. Put on kitchen roll to drain off excess fat and then serve on the plate with the Mujadarra.

❃ The most common mistake with this dish is to add too much or too little water and to stir too much.

Served Mujadarra with a colourful salad on the same plate, not beforehand.

Many in Damascus eat pickled vegetables or a bit of yoghurt with this.

Mother preferred a simple Damascene salad, which she prepared to perfection.

❃ سلطة شامية
Damascene Salad

500 g cucumber
500 g tomatoes
1 Romaine lettuce
2 spring onions
1 bunch flat-leaf parsley
1 small bunch mint
1 bunch radishes
1 garlic clove
1 tbsp vinegar (red wine vinegar)
1 lemon
100 ml olive oil
1 tsp salt
1 pinch of pepper

Wash and if necessary peel the cucumbers (preferably the small thin ones), then chop into small dice. Wash the tomatoes and cut into small pieces. Separate the lettuce leaves, wash and cut into small pieces. Wash the spring onions, discard the green part and chop into tiny pieces. Wash the parsley and mint leaves, and chop. Wash and dice the radishes. Peel the garlic clove, crush and mix with the vinegar, lemon juice and olive oil.

Place everything into a large bowl, mix thoroughly and season with salt and pepper just before serving.

Before I leave our house and return to the alley, I just want to introduce you to my favourite dish. This is no mere recipe. It is the pinnacle of elegance in oriental cuisine. I learned to prepare it from Mother and in the end she let me make it for her. You know what a good cook she was and what high standards she set. My girlfriends also always want me to make this dish for them. I am beginning to believe that I can actually prepare it.

The dish is called *Wara Einab* (Vine Leaves), though older people still often use the Turkish word for 'leaf', *Yaprak*.

Stuffed Vine Leaves can be prepared with meat or for vegetarian consumption. I think both taste good, but in general opinions vary significantly on this. There is a story of two women who argued over which Stuffed Vine Leaves tasted better. They finally agreed to seek the judgement of a wise woman. She answered: 'I praise and condemn no one in absentia.'

Thereupon, each woman prepared her version and took great care over it. In the end, the Vine Leaves were served on two large plates. The 'judge' ate for a while from the one, then for a while from the other, considered her verdict, ate one plate clean, and soon licked all traces from the other as well. 'I don't know,' she said afterwards. 'Each time I wanted to say the one was better, the other would tempt me to taste it again. Children, I do not know. Perhaps you could agree that both are wonderful. But if you cannot come to an agreement, cook both again as deliciously as today and call on me. I would be happy to try once more.'

It remains a matter of personal preference.

By the way, these delectable little rolls are only difficult to make the first time. After that, it can become quite entertaining. To serve four people, you need about one hour 'rolling time' for the dish. I always drink coffee and listen to music (if I am alone) while doing it, or I gossip with my guests about the world. Before we have got as far as relatives three times removed the dish is ready. It is the ingredients that have to be carefully balanced: the rolling soon becomes routine.

❊ ورق عنب باللحم ❊
Vine leaves stuffed with meat

Cooks used to use fresh vine leaves. You take leaves as large as a hand, remove the stalks, wash them thoroughly, blanche them for 2 minutes in boiling water, then let them cool and start with the rolling. These days, however, you can buy very good quality vine leaves in brine.

500 g vine leaves
500 g mince (beef or lamb)
250 g long grain rice
1 tsp salt
½ tsp pepper
1 tsp dried mint
2 tsp thyme
½ tsp cinnamon
2 garlic cloves
100 ml olive oil
50 g butterfat
100 g pine nuts
3 untreated lemons

Remove the vine leaves from the brine and wash thoroughly.

Remove the stalks from the leaves and then sort the leaves into piles – one of whole leaves, the other of fragments or those with holes in them.

Combine the mince and rice. Add the salt, pepper, mint, thyme and cinnamon and stir. Peel and crush the garlic and mix with the olive oil in a small bowl. Add to the rice mixture and stir thoroughly.

Heat the butterfat in a frying pan. Brown (not blacken) the pine nuts in it. Add to the rice and mix.

If you are not going to use the stuffing immediately, chill it until required.

The objective is to roll the vine leaves and stuffing into finger thick cigars. It is easiest to work with vine leaves on a smooth surface. Marble, glass, a large flat platter or wax cloth are ideal. Place the vine leaf with the smooth side down on the work surface. Spread a strip of the stuffing on the bottom half of the leaf. The vine leaf is more or less shaped like a five-pointed star. Fold the right and left sides of the leaf over the stuffing toward the centre. Fold the stem end of the leaf over the stuffing and roll the whole thing up like a cigar toward the leaf's point. The stuffing should be completely enclosed. The leaves are never identical in size and shape, so you have to develop a feeling for the right amount of stuffing and rolling technique. If the leaf tears or fragments open it up again, remove the stuffing and put the leaf aside to use later as covering. Start again with a new leaf in order to make a roll without gaps or tears.

The choice of saucepan is critical for success. It is preferable to use a somewhat shallower, wide saucepan and fill it with only 2–3 layers of vine leaf rolls, rather than using a deeper saucepan of a smaller diameter. The little rolls will cook more consistently if there are fewer layers.

Line the saucepan with the damaged leaves and lay the little *rolls, seam side down, next to each other on top of this lining. Try not to leave any gaps. Press down lightly on the first layer with the flat of your hand. Then place the second layer at a slight angle so no two rolls lie in parallel on top of each other. The second layer should also be placed seam side down. Then continue with the third layer.*

Make certain there are absolutely no bits of rice or meat on the surface of the bundles. If there are any leaves or stuffing left over, roll these up and put them in a smaller pan in the same way. The rice stuffing can also be cooked separately without any vine leaves. You can use any leftover leaves and leaf fragments for covering the rolls.

Wash the lemons and cut into ½ cm thick slices. Then lay the lemon slices on the rolls to cover.

Add sufficient water to just cover the lemon slices.

Place a heat resistant plate upside down on the lemon slices so the rolls do not separate during cooking.

Bring to a boil over high heat, cover and then simmer over low heat for about 30 minutes.

Turn off the heat and allow the vine leaves to rest 5 minutes. Then remove the plate, the lemon slices and covering leaves. Carefully lift the rolls out with spaghetti tongs and serve warm.

A squeeze of lemon goes well with this. Some like to dunk the little rolls in yoghurt; others prefer to enjoy them plain.
Vine Leaves with Vegetarian Stuffing are described later in the book (see page 185).

My childhood girlfriend Samira's family lived about halfway down Abbara Alley until a short while ago. Her mother, now called Granny Nasime, had a difficult life. She lost her parents when she was 11 and, although she was the youngest of the four children, she had to be mother to her three brothers from then on. She boiled, washed and ironed the laundry. She cleaned the house, bought the groceries and took care of the garden. When she was 20 the three brothers finally left home and she met and married a singer. He was a good-looking man. Every member of his family – father, mother and five siblings – was a musician. They performed at weddings and special celebrations. Once in a while they earned some money, but for the most part it was a labour of love, as was typical of those days. In other words: the family was on the breadline.

Because Nasime could neither sing nor play an instrument, she had to care for the entire family, including the 11 children. 'Their appetites were more voracious than a locust and more ungrateful than a hole.' She groans to this day when she thinks back on it. If she had not, in a moment of divine inspiration, refused to sell her parents' house, which her brothers had given her in gratitude, she would have come to a wretched end.

She soon fell pregnant with Samira, later to be my friend. By now she was living in a slum outside the city's Eastern Gate. She had rented out the house in Abbara Alley. It was not unusual for the rent to be the sole source of income for her husband's entire family. Nasime bore all of this with the patience of someone who loves.

Was love really the only source of this strength? No. Damascus looks back on over 8,000 years of culture. This gives its inhabitants a rare ability to get back up after a catastrophe and start over.

Her husband was different. He deserted her and her one-year-old daughter after his first success. He had had a big hit with a cheap war song, appeared on stage everywhere, was interviewed and pretended to be patriotic – exactly what the media wanted. There was big talk about film and theatre. The husband lost his head. One day Nasime discovered that he was living in a grand house with a rich woman. When she confronted him about it, he didn't deny it, nor did he hit her, but instead offered her a job as cleaner for his lover. That was the end. 'Sometimes we can suffer misfortune, but misfortune does not suffer us,' Nasime explained.

She moved out and returned to her parents' house in Abbara Alley. The husband was never to be seen again. By the end he was little more than a heap of alcoholic misery. He died of cirrhosis of the liver.

Nasime began to work as a seamstress and earned a decent living for the first time. Samira grew up to be a marvellous woman, who soon married a doctor and opened a practice with him. Now, there are as many doctors in Damascus as there are grains of sand in the sea, so you have to be something rather special to make a good living. The names of the European universities where a doctor claims to have studied count for more than the quality of his work or his love for his patients. Samira's husband really is a good doctor; but he only read medicine in Damascus. These are the doctors who earn the least when they open their own practices, because they don't like working in a state-run hospital. The practice did not do well. Nevertheless, Samira had four children in four years and shortly after each birth she sent her children to her mother Nasime, who did not have much to do as she was living alone. The young couple picked the children up in the evening, well fed, clean and satisfied, and dropped them off again early the next morning. Nasime was busy twelve hours a day and absolutely shattered by evening. That is why we invited her whenever possible to join us for supper and coffee.

Nasime's son-in-law had to give up his practice a year ago and now works on a large hospital project in Aleppo in the north. When they moved, Grandma Nasime sold her house and followed her daughter, as the children would not go anywhere without their granny.

At the end of its straight stretch, Abbara Alley meets Jew Alley, which has been renamed *Tal al Hijara*, Stone Hill. There are only a few Jewish families remaining in Damascus. More than a thousand Jews used to live here but many have emigrated to America and Israel since the travel ban was lifted in 1992. The life of the Jewish minority was never in danger, but with the ongoing Israeli conflict, their freedom was curtailed and so many left the country as soon as they could.

On the left the alley opens on to two cul-de-sacs that lead to the old city wall. The first cul-de-sac on the right leads to St Paul's Chapel at the place along the wall where Paul was able to flee in a basket. Here you will find the little Bab Kisan Gate as well as the entrance to the bare chapel dedicated to the saint.

In a sense no other church could better represent the character of Saul/Paul than this inconspicuous chapel: strict, ascetic and standing by a wall that separates one world from another. Without Paul, Christianity would have remained a moving Middle Eastern fairy tale about a young revolutionary named Jesus, the first in the world to speak the sentence, 'Love your enemy.'

Memory, or
Of shadow plays and
pugnacious women

Between the beginning of Abbara Alley and its junction with al-Kishle lie a hundred metres full of life and noise. Just before the intersection stands the Suwayd family's house, a masterpiece of times past. At the junction you run into Straight Street again, with Jew Alley on the left, which splits and leads to Abbara on the left and the centre of the Old City on the right.

Aside from a few cul-de-sacs, all paths in the Old City lead to any given point. The many different cultures that have lived within its walls may have lived separate lives, but there have never been ghettos.

On the right from the crossing you come to the heart of the Christian Quarter – Bab Touma Street. This street leads to the second city gate, which is named for it: Bab Touma or Thomas Gate. It is a distinguished street. Not 50 metres from the crossing stands the used to be the girls' school, a small convent school, governed by Armenian Catholic nuns. Do you remember? I went went to school there as well.

The Armenians came to Syria fleeing massacres of their people and have lived amongst us ever since. They are well respected for their industriousness and directness. Many of them are precision mechanics, watchmakers, car mechanics or goldsmiths.

On the right of the convent is al-Misq Alley, which we have already wandered down. Nearby, on the right hand side of Bab Touma Street, is

41

the Syrian Orthodox community's church. On the left are several houses and shops that are not particularly attractive, and then the alley climbs steeply up hill. This street was once called *Sifil a-Talle*, at the foot of the hill, but now it is known as St John of Damascus Alley. John of Damascus lived in the seventh century. He was a major figure in the history of Christian theology who was also known for the brilliance of his preaching, earning himself the name John Chrysorrheas (literally, 'golden stream'). Our father owned a valuable, handwritten 19th-century copy of his work, which he often read from and guarded like a jewel.

St John of Damascus alley takes you past several historic mosques, hammams and churches of the Qaimariyya quarter, eventually leading to the Umayyad Mosque. But for now, let us stay on the Bab Touma. There was a second girls' school near the beginning of Sifil a-Talle Alley: the school of the Besançon nuns, where my friend Josephine went to school. She comes from Egypt and all the members of her family are Christian Copts. As you know, the Copts are amongst the earliest Christians; it was also they who caused the first schism in the Church, when the nature of Jesus was at issue. The argument arose from a delicate question: Is Jesus of one or two natures? Is he man and god simultaneously – 'the word of God made flesh' – or did he have two natures, that is, was he a man *and* a god? This was debated at length in 451 AD. Most eastern Christians believed in the one nature, while the majority of the European churchmen at the meeting could not imagine something so complex and voted for the two cleanly separable and easily understandable natures co-existing in one person.

The so-called Monophysites, that is, those who believed in the single nature of Jesus, split from the Church. The supporters of this view are called Copts in Egypt and Jacobites in Syria. The official church in Byzantium (later called Constantinople and later still Istanbul) persecuted and tormented them for a long time, but the Egyptians remained loyal to their local church. Neither Byzantium, nor Rome, nor Athens was able to exert significant influence there. In Syria, on account of its proximity to Jerusalem and Byzantium, the story is more complicated. The Syrian

Christians went through several more splits and some sects later merged with the church in Rome.

Josephine's father is called Salman. He is a pious Christian and a member of virtually every church organisation. This annoyed Josephine as a young girl because she could not go anywhere in the quarter without running into her father's pious acquaintances. If she was eating an ice-lolly on the street, before she had finished she would always bump into at least three gentlemen who would nod meaningfully and purse their lips, because Josephine was from a genteel, though poor, family, in which it was not considered proper to eat an ice-lolly in public.

Her father, Salman, had seven children. Thanks to his membership in numerous Christian organisations, he was able to send each and every one to the best schools – at no cost, of course. Today, his children are well-known engineers, doctors and teachers. Josephine is the director of the children's clinic and well loved, not only because she is an important woman in her field, but because she has the soul of a clown. All the mothers always want to go to the friendly Egyptian woman.

Salman was clearly shrewd not just about the afterlife, but even more so in relation to this life on earth. With his income as a chef in the then luxury hotel Samir Amis he would not have been able to afford the education of even one child.

Salman cooked everything well, but when I and Josephine's other girlfriends visited her home we always wanted his Falafel. There were none tastier in Damascus. And he was always happy to be able to satisfy his children's friends for so little money.

❋ فلافل ❋

Falafel
Deep-fried ground chickpeas
500 g dried broad beans (US: fava beans)
250 g dried chickpeas (US: garbanzo beans)
1 bunch parsley
4 garlic cloves

3 large onions
2 tbsp salt
1 tsp allspice
1 tsp ground coriander
1 tsp pepper
1 tsp ground cumin
1 tsp cinnamon
2 tbsp flour
1 tsp baking powder
100 g sesame seeds, peeled but not roasted
Oil for frying

Thoroughly wash the broad beans and chickpeas, and soak in plenty of water for at least 12 hours. Allow the beans to drain and run through a meat grinder or finely chop in a food processor. Place in a large bowl. Wash the parsley and blend the leaves together with the peeled garlic cloves and peeled and quartered onions in the meat grinder or food processor. Place in the bowl. Add the salt, spices (except sesame seeds), flour and baking powder to the bowl, mix thoroughly and run through the meat grinder or food processor again until a fine, smooth purée develops. Leave the purée to rest covered for two hours and then mix thoroughly again.

Put generous amounts of frying oil in a deep saucepan and heat to ca. 200° C/400°F/Gas Mark 6. The oil must be at least 5–7 cm deep so the Falafel do not touch the bottom.

Spread the sesame seeds on a smooth large plate.

Form little balls or sausages from the purée with the help of a spoon; briefly roll them in the sesame seeds and glide into the oil. You can also form the little patties with wet hands.

Put the Falafel in the oil next to each other as rapidly as possible until they are close together (but not on top of each *other), covering the surface of the oil. Fry to a golden brown for about four minutes, turning them with a slotted spoon. Remove and drain on a piece of kitchen towel.*

Falafel should be eaten warm and are usually served with salads, yoghurt, sumac, tahini, radishes, tomatoes, cucumbers, paprika and lemon juice.

❀ *You can vary the ratio between the broad beans and the chickpeas. You can also make Falafel without broad beans and only chickpeas and the other ingredients. But the recipe described here is the best.*

Not far from where Josephine lives is a famous house, the most beautiful in the Christian quarter: the house of Anton Shamiyya – a wealthy Christian who enjoyed life and tried to create a paradise within his four walls. He completed the house in 1866 and 32 years later the German Kaiser Wilhelm II stayed there during his visit to Damascus.

But back to Bab Touma Street. If you continue north, towards the gate, you will pass the seat of the Lazarists, a Catholic congregation from France, founded by St Vincent de Paul in 1625, which to this day supports several missions around the world. Two of their cloisters are here in Bab Touma and still in operation – one for nuns and one for priests – but the Lazarists' elite school, one of three elite schools in Damascus, has been nationalised and one does not learn much there any more. Just beyond the curve in the street, on the right hand side, is Lazarist Alley, which leads to the school and convent and finally, if you carry on far enough, will take you back to the Eastern Gate, where we have already visited.

My friend Madhya lives near the top of Lazarist Alley. I enjoy visiting her because she is a fantastical storyteller. She can embellish even the most boring incident to the extent that it becomes an exciting story. I have the feeling Madhya fibs a bit sometimes when she is relating a story. But so what – fibbing is like cooking. Well lied is like well spiced, not too much and not too little.

She probably inherited her talent for telling stories from her father.

He was a gifted storyteller. He had a famous shadow theatre until his death at the end of the 1960s and his hand-painted leather puppets still hang in Madhya's flat.

His props were a white bed sheet, a lamp and his curious puppets that he moved in front of the light source with long poles. Their shadows, together with his voice and other sounds, would set the scene for an entire play.

The art of shadow puppetry has been known in the Middle East since the days of the Pharaohs. They experienced their golden age in India, but were well loved in the Arab world. The Ottoman Sultan Salim discovered the art form in Damascus and Cairo when he conquered Arabia. He enjoyed it so much that he took several artists back to Istanbul, his capital to entertain his son. That is how he became one of the greatest patrons of the art of shadow puppetry.

For the most part, the plays dealt with people's common life. The stories were funny, though frequently stuffed with morality, which did not seem to detract from their appeal. The plays flowed into people's lives and became a theme of their mundane existence. And the storyteller would draw ideas from everyday life, weaving in current issues that were of particular concern to his audience.

Advertising for certain businesses would also make an appearance in the shadow plays. Suddenly one of the characters would begin praising the dishes served in a certain restaurant or admire the furnishings of another establishment and request the address of the eatery or of the joiner. A second character would then name them for the audience. Madhya claimed her father covered half of his expenses with such adverts.

Madhya's father made all his own puppets, wrote the plays and provided the voices for four to five different characters in every performance. A shadow player has to be able to make music, sing and whistle and her father knew over 70 songs by heart. He would move the puppets with his right hand, while his left hand and feet played musical instruments and operated incredibly complex props that made various noises – walking, running, wind, water and animal sounds – to accompany the dialogue.

Once, when he gave a performance for some foreign diplomats, they could not believe there was only one person sat behind the screen and were deeply impressed by his artistry when they confirmed that there was.

He became very famous and made the most of his fame. He would tell stories in instalments. The hero of his stories, who was usually fighting for justice, was extremely popular with the audience, so much so that they would hurry to the café on the following evening to hear the next episode. When Madhya's father realised just how much his hero had captured people's imagination, he began to blackmail his audience. As soon as they had quietened down in order to hear the next chapter, the puppeteer would begin to cough. Absolute silence. Then he would step out in front of the screen and say, 'I am very sorry, but the hero of the story has been taken ill; he cannot come today. Perhaps the gentlemen would give some money so I can take a gift to him and convince him to come by anyway.'

You might expect that this would be met with boos and hisses, and that the audience would have departed in hordes. But nothing of the sort happened. People meekly collected the money. Only then did he continue the tale, though not of course before the main character had thanked the audience for their donation and God for his mercy – his voice hoarse as he did so.

Madhya cooks quite a bit. Her chicken dishes are amongst the very best in Damascus. You should know that in Arabia chickens, cockerels, doves and all other small fowl were once a luxury. In many folktales, stories, anecdotes and jokes, 'eating chicken' was a symbol of endless riches.

※ دجاج مع أرضي شوكي ※

Chicken breast with artichokes

1 garlic clove
Salt and pepper
2 tbsp white wine vinegar
2 tbsp medium hot mustard
1 tsp oregano

500 g chicken breast (skinned and boned)
50 ml sunflower oil
5–6 artichoke hearts

Peel the garlic clove, crush with a bit of salt, then mix with
the vinegar, mustard, oregano, and pepper. Set aside. Cut the
chicken breast in strips, 2 cm long and ½ cm thick. Place the oil
in a briefly preheated pan and fry the chicken until crispy.
Remove the artichoke hearts from the tin, drain, quarter and
add to the pan. Fry for 5 minutes, then stir in the sauce, cover
and leave to simmer on low heat for 10 minutes.

❈ Rice or potatoes generally go well with chicken. Madhya
always prepares a large quantity of baked 'golden potatoes'.

❈ البطاطا الذهبية

Golden Potatoes

1 kg medium-sized firm cooking potatoes
1 tsp salt
100 ml sunflower oil
100 g butterfat

Wash and peel the potatoes (it's a shame to lose the vitamins, but
it can't be helped), then place in boiling salted water and blanche
for 5 minutes. Allow to dry for just over 7 minutes. Put the oil
and butterfat on a baking tray (or oven-proof dish) and preheat
in the oven at 250° C/475° F/Gas Mark 9. When the butterfat
has melted, add the potatoes and turn to coat a few times. Roast
in the oven for about 20 minutes. Turn the potatoes repeatedly
so they crisp on all sides.

The tray or dish must be large enough for the potatoes to fit
side-by-side and not on top of each other.
You can also thoroughly wash the potatoes, halve them and cook

them in their skins in the oven without blanching them first.
However, they will take a bit longer this way.

❋ فروج مـع الثوم ❋

Chicken Breast with Garlic and Coriander

100 g butterfat or sunflower oil
1 medium onion
500 g chicken breast
1 lemon
3 large garlic cloves
50 ml olive oil
1 tsp each salt, allspice and ground coriander

This dish tastes equally good whether using butterfat or oil for
frying. Place the fat or oil in a preheated pan. As soon as it is
hot, add the roughly diced onion and fry to golden brown over
medium heat. Remove from the pan. The fat will be reused.

Wash and dry the chicken breast. Cut into small dice or strips.
Fry in the fat until it is crispy, then douse with the juice of
a lemon and reduce heat to its lowest level. Add the onion,
crushed garlic, olive oil, salt and spices. Stir once. Cover and let
simmer for 5 minutes. Stir once more and serve warm.
The best part of this dish is the spicy sauce. Serve with bread.

Neighbourhood, or
Of life between the Spanish crown
and hearty soups

If you return to Bab Touma Street from Madhya's alley, you will notice that from the top of the alley the street is packed with shops and elegant houses. Most of the buildings, however, are less than 150 years old, because the area almost completely burned down in 1860, the year of the pogroms.

Georges Diab, owner of a legendary coffee house in the new city, lived directly across from the alley until his death in August 2001. The name of the coffee house was Café Havana and was the meeting place for Damascene intellectuals and journalists, a marketplace for news and rumours. It witnessed the rise and fall of many authors and journalists, who travelled on fortune's wheel from starving intellectual to influential minister and back again.

Again and again Georges Diab mediated between high-ranking functionaries and those who had fallen from grace. He would remind the newly powerful, in a friendly and circumspect manner, that the poor devil had played backgammon, chess or cards with His Excellency only a short time ago and how they had laughed together. It was not unusual for him to be successful in his missions where other, far more powerful intermediaries had failed.

Not far from Madhya's alley, across from Bulad Alley, is an unusual looking house: the house of the Spanish Crown. A marble plaque in

Spanish is mounted above the door. The house was built in 1908 with public funds from the Spanish capital Madrid and was the seat of the Spanish Consul under the Ottomans. Later the house went into private ownership but the marble ornamentation bears witness to this day to its earlier beauty.

Bab Touma exudes a peculiarly urban flair. The architectural style of the houses lining the street is distinctively European as most of the magnificent buildings were built during the time of the French Occupation (1920–1945). As a result, tourists and guidebooks pay scant attention to this area. Bear in mind that Bab Touma Street and its surrounding alleys are the heart of the Christian Quarter.

A certain lack of interest on the part of European travellers is understandable. Not only are the religion, customs and houses in this area not very exotic due to their close affinity with Europe, even the *Souq*, the oriental market that is a characteristic feature of Arab cities, is more chaotic than oriental. The shops in the Bab Touma Souq are jumbled up next to each other with little regard for atmosphere: a video store stands across from a fast food place and a chemist is next to a grocer. There are several bakeries (one of which has belonged to our family for over sixty years), flower shops, electrical goods and grocery stores next to cheap oriental general stores. In other words, the street is arranged in a European style. In contrast, when you consider the spice bazaar, *al Bzouriyya*, you can begin to understand why the guidebooks give Bab Touma Street only marginal attention. But, the travel guides show only one face of the area, overlooking the many fascinating characters that still inhabit the area and the several outstanding houses and churches this street has to offer.

One of the surprises of the Christian Quarter, for example, is a tiny mosque of unpretentious architecture, built as recently as 1965. Almost next to it is the beautiful Franciscan Monastery, which the Damascenes refer to as the Latin Monastery (by which people here mean European Catholic). The alley that leads from the main street along the monastery's walls to the eastern city wall and the Eastern Gate is also called Monastery Alley. Almost opposite the Franciscan Monastery is a small church belonging to the Maronites, a tiny minority sect amongst Syrian Christians.

The Nadshars live not far from the Maronite Church. They have two children who are proof that life is full of miracles. The couple must be the most simple-minded and quarrelsome two people on earth. The woman was a washerwoman in a hospital; the man was discharged from the army for laziness and being too contentious. He was unsuited for repair work or messenger duty – all far too complicated for him – but the Catholic Church finally found a job that was absolutely perfect for such a surly man. After all, a great entrance to a Patriarch's seat looks far more impressive if a man in a foul mood guards it.

Yet their sons are a miracle. There's no other way of describing it, not without consigning every book of pedagogy and psychology to the fire. However it happened, the two boys grew up to be bright, peace-loving men. The older one became a doctor, heart and soul; his brother an aircraft engineer. Both later left the country and now live happily with their wives and children in the United States. They send their parents money from there – and they are not mean about it either.

In spite of their moods, I enjoy visiting the old couple and am amused by their constant squabbles. After all, when two fighting cocks are over 70, their malice can only seem funny. I have a good laugh and the two are usually reconciled – until their next argument.

However irate Mr Nadshar becomes, though, I can always coax him into agreeing with me by asking him who cooks the best soups in Damascus. 'Na'ime, my wife, naturally,' he immediately responds and practically drools at the thought.

And, indeed, Na'ime cooks lovely soups. I wrote down her best a long time ago.

٭ شوربة أرضي شوكي ٭
Artichoke Soup

10 artichoke hearts
4 large tomatoes

2 medium onions
100 ml olive oil
2 tbsp freshly squeezed lemon juice
3 garlic cloves
1 tsp salt
1 tsp ground cardamom
1 bunch fresh parsley

You can use either fresh artichoke hearts or those tinned in brine. If you use the fresh ones, remove all the tough outer leaves, then trim off the top third of the leaves, as well as the tough outer part of the heart including the stem. Rub the cut surfaces of the bottom and leaves with lemon. Then scoop out the choke, which covers the heart, with a small spoon. Wash the hearts and rub again with lemon. Cook until done in boiling water for 30–40 minutes; then lift out, allow to cool and quarter. Tinned artichokes need just to be thoroughly rinsed under running water and then quartered.

Wash the tomatoes and dice. Peel the onions and dice. Heat the oil in a saucepan and fry the onions in it. Add 1 l water. Then add the artichokes, lemon juice, tomatoes, crushed garlic clove, salt and cardamom and allow to cook for 10 minutes. Sprinkle with finely chopped parsley.

Serve with white bread.

❀ A number of friends have served this soup with minor variations. Instead of tomatoes, they cut chicken breast or tender beef into small pieces, cook it in 1 l water for 30 minutes and then add the meat and broth to the onions.

Whether with beef or chicken, or vegetarian, this soup tastes wonderful when you add 1 tbsp cream to each soup bowl just before serving.

All the neighbours still delight in telling the story of the young officer who was a lodger in the Nadshar's house several years ago. The young man was from the North and had to spend six months in Damascus to continue his education. He rented a room on the first floor and he was even willing to put up with the constant arguments because it reminded him of home where his parents were also constantly at each other's throats.

One day, upon returning to the house, he smelled a tantalising scent coming from the kitchen. He timidly inquired whether he might be able to share a plate with them. Mrs Nadshar knew how miserly her husband was and hesitated. As the officer was aware of this, he quickly added, 'Of course, I would pay for it.' Thus was he given his first plate of Arnabiyye.

From that moment on his fate was sealed. He became addicted to this soup and wanted it five days a week. (To his annoyance, he had to spend the other two nights a week in barracks.) He was an unusual man, Mrs Nadshar said. He knew even as a young officer that he would not take long to make general, and he soon did, but even then he would come at least once a week to eat Arnabiyye. Mrs Nadshar's word was holy as far as he was concerned. He never denied her a request. Often these were petitions from neighbours to make the lives of their children, who were doing mandatory service in the military, a bit easier. He granted her every wish without asking for anything in return, aside from the Arnabiyye of course.

✳ أرنبية ✳

Arnabiyye
Swiss Chard, Lentil and Sumac Soup

300 g brown lentils
1 kg swiss chard (silver beet)
50 g coarsely ground burghul
50 g flour
1 large onion
50 ml olive oil
3 garlic cloves

1 tsp salt
100 g sumac powder
1 tsp ground coriander
1 tsp ground cumin

Soak the burghul for 10 minutes and then combine with the flour and a bit of water into a coarse dough. Take a small piece of dough between damp hands and roll into a small ball. Repeat until you have used up the dough. Place the balls on a plate next to each other without touching.

Wash the lentils and bring to the boil in a large pot with 2 l water. Thoroughly wash the Swiss chard, remove the leaves from the stems and separately cut into 1 cm pieces. Peel and finely chop the onion. Fry to a golden brown in preheated oil in a large pan. Add the chopped stems and steam for 5 minutes, then add in the leaves and fry for another 5 minutes. Peel, crush and add the garlic. Stir thoroughly. Let it all cool a little and then add everything, including the frying oil, to the boiling lentils. Add salt, sumac, coriander and cumin, and let simmer over low heat for about 10 minutes. Add the dough balls to the simmering soup, cook for another 5 minutes and serve hot.

Serve with toasted bread.

Our bakery is in Bab Touma Street. It has never been particularly attractive. In general, the old bakeries in Damascus are ugly, functional, carelessly designed buildings. This only began to change in the mid-sixties when modern bakeshops began to open with more attractive facades, sales counters and display cases. Marble and glass, wood and steel were tastefully incorporated. At the same time, however, as the bakeries became more automated, the individuality of the products on offer was lost. The craft of baking bread hardly exists anymore. The workers in the bakeries are capable of running the machines, but when the electricity fails, they are at a loss.

Bread plays a central role in Arab food habits and Damascenes are famous for their fussy and frequently arrogant attitude to the quality of their bread. As I mentioned before, they will not touch day old bread: our bakers have had to work seven-day weeks for centuries. A touch too dark or too light, too crisp or too soft, and everyone, rich or poor, turns up their nose.

Our bakery stopped making bread because it no longer made economic sense. It now only produces pastries and delicacies to order, which are still in demand but which people don't want to bake at home anymore. The most popular amongst these specialities is S'fiha.

The word means dish or flat disc and is an exact description of these little pizzas that Damascenes adore. S'fiha ranks alongside tabbouleh, kibbeh, kebab and stuffed vine leaves as one of the best dishes with which to spoil your guests.

Of course there are many variations, and lovely accompaniments, such as a simple meat topping, which is baked on a round of dough and called Lahma bi Ajeen – the name reminds us of the origin of the well-known Turkish Lahmacun.

The size of the base increases the more commercial the S'fiha becomes. The ideal diameter is 8 to 10 centimetres. Once it reaches 20 cm, you have to question whether you are still getting a S'fiha.

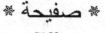

S'fiha
Mini flat breads with meat, pine nuts, yoghurt and pomegranate juice mixture as topping
The bread dough is prepared as described on Page 26.

The Classic Topping
4 large onions
500 g beef mince
1 garlic clove

200 g yoghurt

2 tbsp pomegranate syrup (or you can substitute 1 tbsp balsamic
vinegar and 1 tbsp sumac)

1 tsp salt

1 tsp pepper

1 tsp ground coriander

1 tsp dried thyme

1 tsp cinnamon

½ ground nutmeg

50 g pine nuts

50 g butterfat

Peel the onions, finely dice and add to the meat in a bowl. Peel
the garlic, crush and add. Add the yoghurt, pomegranate syrup,
salt and spices and mix.

Pomegranate syrup can be obtained from almost any Arab
grocery. Alternatively you can take fresh, preferably fairly sour
pomegranates and squeeze the juice from the seeds. You should
not use the hard seeds, as they tend to compromise the flavour.
If you cannot get pomegranates, mix 1 tbsp balsamic vinegar
with 1 tbsp sumac.

Lightly brown the pine nuts in butterfat until they are honey
coloured. Then add them along with the butterfat to the meat
mixture.

Chill the mixture in the refrigerator for 1 hour. Then squeeze
out the excess liquid with your hands.

Place the mixture in a clean bowl.

Prepare the bread dough as previously described.

Shape pieces of the dough into the size of tennis balls. Roll
them out on a floured surface with a rolling pin to 2 to 3 mm
thickness. Cut out rounds of 8 to 10 cm diameter using a glass
or scone cutter. Knead the scraps back into the rest of the dough.

Place 1 tbsp of the mixture in the middle of each round and distribute evenly leaving a 5 mm gap at the edge.

Place the S'fihas on an oiled or lightly floured baking tray. Preheat the oven to 250° C/475° F/Gas Mark 9.

The rounds need to be pressed down all over with the fingertips before going in the oven. This prevents air bubbles from forming or bursting. Avoid tearing any holes in the dough.

Bake for 5 minutes on the bottom rack, then 10 minutes on the middle rack until the dough and topping are crispy and brown.

S'fiha is eaten immediately and very hot. The bakeries have a high capacity and can rapidly produce great quantities of S'fiha that are delivered to customers in the immediate vicinity within a few minutes by messenger boys.

If you make S'fiha at home (never for more than 4 people as you need to count on 8–10 pieces per person), then the cook and host should serve the guests directly from the oven to their plates (without forgetting your own) and always make sure that people get a second helping.

If you like, serve S'fiha with a spoonful of yoghurt for dipping. Mixed salads also go well with it. In this case you do not eat the salad first, but with the S'fiha. The salad increases the appetite.

In addition to this posh S'fiha there is another popular variety that Damascenes particularly enjoy for breakfast or as an appetiser. It is simple to make and the slices are also often served as an accompaniment to other dough-based dishes.

If you have some S'fiha dough left over, but no topping mixture, use the spice mixture Zahtar (see page 187), which is in every Damascene home. Mix it with olive oil, spread it on the dough surface and bake it. This makes for some quick appetizer titbits.

The Arabic name Mnaqush, plural Mnaquish, means painted or etched, simply because, before it goes in the oven, the dough has to be pressed down with the fingertips (without making any holes) so that no air bubbles develop.

✲ مناقيش بالزعتر ✲

Mnaquish bi zahtar
Bread with olive oil and zahtar

Roll out the bread or yeast dough and cut into portions of whatever shape you desire. Brush with a mixture of zahtar and olive oil. Lightly press down all the dough pieces with your fingertips and bake in an oven preheated to 200° C/400° F/Gas Mark 6. Bake the bread for 5 minutes on the lowest rack, then 10 minutes on the middle rack.

Be careful, as like all herbs Zahtar tends to char quickly. Take the tray out of the oven as soon as the dough is a crispy brown.

A family, whose daughter married the grandson of the ingenious Fares Churi, lives across from our bakery. The young man is also called Fares. His grandfather was an important poet, a courageous solicitor, and, most important of all, a politician of world renown. He held many political posts during the French Occupation and later became the Chief of Delegation during the negotiations for independence and drove the French crazy with his brilliant ideas and his charm. One of the most famous stories tells of when Fares Churi arrived at an international conference with his small delegation and sat on the chairs where the French usually sat. Syria was still occupied. The French got upset and demanded that the Syrians get up immediately and vacate their seats. Fares Churi remained calm. He turned to the journalists who had rushed there and spoke the following words in perfect English: 'My dear ladies and gentlemen. The French cannot tolerate it if a Syrian occupies their chairs for five minutes; yet they have occupied our country for 25 years and are surprised that we are protesting!'

Bakri Alley is a few metres along Bab Touma Street on the left and contains a large Jesuit church and a hammam that was very important for the inhabitants of our Quarter. Hammam Bakri dates from the 16th century and positively clings to the side of a little mosque from the 11th century. Its entrance is directly under the minaret. Our grandfather on our father's side went to this hammam every week. He liked the atmosphere and met with his friends there.

Not far from Hammam Bakri, until about 10 years ago, stood Adnan's butcher shop. Adnan was the most famous butcher in the entire Quarter. He came from Aleppo and was basically a charmer who was always telling the women what they wanted to hear. That's why people, or more precisely women, queued up in front of his shop. He supposedly had clever hands and great taste. Mother laughed about it all her life. 'That man certainly has clever hands. Before you know it he's switched the good piece of meat that he just cut from the lamb or mutton and showed you with something worse.' The part about great taste, however, was quite true: his kebabs were second to none. In general, the Aleppines are the best in the Middle East when it comes to preparing kebab. Neither Turks, nor Syrians, nor Greeks nor Lebanese can do it better. In Aleppo, Roman, Greek, Turkish, Armenian and Indian cooking traditions melted together.

Adnan the butcher even seduced an orientalist from Florida with his charms. She was a tall blond woman of exceptional beauty, but with a terrible accent. She succumbed to the man when she bought a Kebab sandwich from him. They married and, when the orientalist was finished with her studies, Adnan moved to Florida, where he opened a Kebab restaurant. His successor in the butcher shop is a competent and proper man, but unfortunately he does not have the charm of that fox, Adnan.

❋ كباب ❋
Kebab
Skewers with mince-herb mixture
The meat paste for this dish is the starting point, with minor
variations, for an array of hearty dishes that are very popular in
Damascus and known as kufteh, kefteh, kufta, or kofta.

The Meat Mixture
3 medium onions
1 large bunch of parsley
2 garlic cloves
1 kg mince (beef or lamb; not lean, preferably fatty)
1 tsp salt
1 tsp pepper
1 tsp paprika
1 tsp cinnamon
½ ground nutmeg

Peel and quarter the onions. Wash the parsley and remove the
large stems. Peel the garlic. Combine onions, parsley and garlic
with the meat and run through a meat grinder or food processor.
Add the salt, pepper, paprika, cinnamon and nutmeg and mix
thoroughly. Chill for half an hour in the refrigerator.

With damp hands, form the mixture into little balls and
thread them on flat metal skewers, forming them into an 8–10
cm long sausage. Keep lightly squeezing the meat on the skewer
so it stays in place.

Heat the coals on a grill (you can also use an electric grill, of
course) until they are glowing and put the skewers on the grill
about 10 cm above the coals, cooking them until they turn
brown. Keep turning them. If necessary, brush them lightly
with sunflower oil.

You can also shape the mixture into finger thick sausages and fry them in a pan.

A mixed salad goes well with this.

❋ If you have difficulty getting the meat mixture to stick to the skewer, add an egg and about 150 g bread that has been soaked (without crusts) to the meat mixture and knead through.

Those who, like the inhabitants of Aleppo, love their food spicy may add ½ tsp cayenne pepper to the meat mixture.

❋ كفتـة بالصينية

Kofta with potatoes or tomatoes on a baking tray

1 kg firm cooking potatoes and/or
1 kg beef tomatoes
150 pine nuts
2 tbsp tomato paste
Butterfat

Mix the tomato paste and golden brown roasted pine nuts into the Kebab meat mixture and knead thoroughly.

Grease a baking tray with the butterfat. With wet hands, place the meat mixture in the middle of the tray and smooth it out into an even layer no more than 2 to 3 cm thick.

Bake in an oven preheated to 250° C/475° F/Gas Mark 9 until crispy, about 25 minutes.

Remove the tray from the oven and cut pieces based on the shape of the tray (with a round tray, cut triangular pieces like slices of cake; with a square or rectangular tray, you would cut squares).

Only now are the potatoes and/or tomatoes placed on the top.

First parboil the potatoes until almost soft, then peel and slice.

Coat in sunflower oil and distribute decoratively on the meat.

Or, wash and slice the tomatoes and distribute like the potatoes.

You can also use both, topping the meat with alternate layers of tomato and potato.

Then return the tray to the oven and bake for another 15 minutes (preferably with the heat coming from the top, like from a grill).

Serve with rice or bread; a green salad is a must.

Sounds of the Streets

'Can you hear the cries of the hawkers in the background?' asked Marie, and kept quiet while I listened, but I strained to make out what the old man with the tremulous voice was selling. The telephone connection wasn't very good that day. Later on, I told my sister about it. She laughed: 'That must have been Omar, singing the praises of his cucumbers. You remember Omar, don't you? And without waiting for an answer, she went on: 'He's an old man now, with white hair, He's been supplying the people in our alley with vegetables for the past forty years,. As soon as he arrives, he calls out a couple of times and the women descend like locusts on the panniers on his horse. His veg and salad leaves are famous for their freshness and taste. He charges more than the expensive greengrocers, sometimes twice as much as the other street traders, but people still prefer buying from him. It's his special brand of charm that does it. He's always got a little homily ready for his customers. He knows all the children by name and comes up with a funny quip in response to anything you ask him. Just like his veg, the quality of his patter hasn't declined over the years.'

Many things may have changed in Damascus, but not the lyrical, often witty cries of the street vendors. A standard ploy is to name-check the areas where the fruit and veg (allegedly) come from, because these places, with their favourable weather conditions, are a surefire guarantee of the quality of the produce in question.

Apples: *Each and every one of my apples is like a beautiful, blushing cheek.*
or: *All my apples are from Izmir/the Lebanon/Sabadani!*
or: *My apples are as sweet as candies, sugar and muscat wine!*
Scarcely any other fruit has as much praise heaped on it as the apple.

Apricots: *Melts in the mouth!*
or: *My apricots taste like they're filled with rose water!*
or: *Once you taste them, you'll forget the price!*
or: *You were brought down by wind, just as I was brought down by greed!*
This last, cryptic cry needs some explanation. Ripe apricots are knocked off the tree by high winds, and the trader complains that greed ruined him and made him into a poor street vendor. And so he addresses the apricot as a brother in misfortune.

Aubergines: *Oh aubergine, blacker than the night!*
or: *My aubergines are like meat to the poor!*

Barasik (Butter biscuits covered in sesame seeds): *My Barasik are food for the swallows!*

Beans (fresh, green): *My beans are from Malta/Bludan!*
or: *Eat them now or dry them for the winter!*
Even today, despite the advent of freezers, many Damascus residents still dry out green beans to preserve them for the winter.

Beetroot: *My beets are the best remedy for a cough!*
or: *Beetroots, plump and ripe!*
or: *Come closer if you're cold!*
Beetroots are boiled before eating, but as this is a long and costly business, people prefer to buy them ready-cooked. It's cheaper to get them from vendors who have carts with pots kept simmering on gas rings, and who sell the beetroot freshly cooked but unpeeled.

Carrots: *Their juice is good for your healtht!*
or: *Dessert for poor widows (or angry mothers-in-law)!*
A rather suggestive double-entendre, this last one!!

Chick peas: (toasted chick peas are a favourite Syrian snack):
Chick peas – tattooed, soft and warm!
and: *Go on, splash out tonight, Barmakid!*
This is one of the strangest cries you'll hear. The first part is an accurate description, as chick peas really do take on an attractive dark pattern on their yellow flesh–rather like a tattoo–when they're roasted. And straight out of the frying pan, they are indeed warm and soft. But in addition, because chick peas are feminine in gender, the vendor's cry also sounds like a man eulogising his lover. The second cry, which sometimes follows the first, is simply meant to convey the idea that chick peas are dirt-cheap and that you can afford to treat your friends to them. But the seller doesn't say that straight out. Instead, he says *Go on, splash out tonight*, and calls the buyer a Barmakid. The Barmakids were high officials of Persian origin in the early years of the Abbasid Caliphate, and were one of the most powerful families in Baghdad. On the orders of the fifth caliph, Harun al-Rashid (ruled 786–809), they were stripped of their power and massacred, after having faithfully served both him and his father. During their lifetime, the Barmakids were known for their fabulously lavish hospitality. The vendor's cry alludes satirically, almost heretically, to this bit of history.

Courgettes: *My courgettes are related to asparagus!*
This is meant to convey the slimness of the vegetables in question.

Cucumbers: *Just like kids' fingers!*
Stressing how tender and dainty the vendor's produce is.

Dates: *My dates come straight from Baghdad!*
Nowadays, thanks to stiff competition from a wide variety of sweets, dates no longer rule the roost. Once upon a time, they were the sweetest thing

to be had in Arabia. The Prophet Mohammed himself, no less, sang their praises.

Figs: *Dew nests in you, figs!*
or: *Pure honey, my figs!*
or: *Bees commit suicide out of envy for you, figs!*
or: *White Baal-figs!*

The best, sweetest figs come from trees that haven't been watered by human hand. In Syria, all fields that aren't watered by artificial irrigation are called 'Baal-fields'. Farmers sow various crops there and just hope that the heavens will smile on them and provide enough rain – a precious commodity in the Middle East. For the ancient civilisations of the Levant, Ba'al was the god of the sky and fertility (the city of Baalbek is named after him).

Yields tend to be low in this arid part of the world, but the fruit that is produced is renowned for its quality, because of its slow rate of growth and the abundant sun it gets while ripening.

Garlic and onions: *Cheaper than scrounging from your neighbour!*

Lemons: *Lemons – medicine for the sick!*
This cry comes from the fact that the Arabic term for insane – *Majnun* – rhymes with *Laimun* (lemon).

Mulberries: *My mulberries will cleanse your blood and wash away your cares!*
or: *Picked fresh with the morning dew on them!*

Oranges: *Fine oranges from Jaffa!*

Pistachios: *No empty shells among my pistachios!*
or: *Pistachios direct from Aleppo!*
Pistachios are usually eaten roasted and salted, but also straight from the

tree. The best ones come from Aleppo. The southernmost point where they are grown commercially is the village of Malula (around 60 km north of Damascus). South of this, trees yield only very few, inferior quality nuts.

Peaches: *The man who first planted you is now safe in God's bosom!* This cry hints at the region's long tradition of growing fruit.
or: *Peaches – the dessert of kings!*

Plums/damsons: *The fruit that doctors would recommend to their sons!*
or: *Your flesh is as dark as ink!*

Potatoes: *Don't ruin a dish of expensive meat with bad potatoes!*
or: *My potatoes are from Yabrud!*
or: *These aren't potatoes – they're truffles!*

Prickly pears: *My prickly pears were grown in Mozzeh!*
or: *Cool, sweet prickly pear – refreshes your heart!*

Quinces: *Quinces – a hiccup after every bite!*
or: *You come from a noble line, o quince!*

Raisins: *The date's brother-in-law – my raisins taste as sweet as honey!*

Salad leaves: *Only God is immortal!*
This cry, one of the most philosophical you'll hear, comes from a time before veg was grown in hothouses. In those days, the salad season in Damascus was very short. Nowadays you can get salad all year round– but the downside is that it all tastes bland.

Spinach: *Soft as a goat's ears!*

Sus (**licorice-root drink**): This refreshing drink, a firm favourite in

Damascus, is made by soaking ground licorice roots in water for a long time. It's served ice-cold.

Sus – makes your pupils black and your cheks red!

Tarragon: *Tarragon, you traitor!*
or: *God punish the traitor!*
or: *This traitorous son of a whore!*
Tarragon's the only herb to stand accused of treachery! It supposedly earned this reputation through its habit of not confining itself to growing where you planted it, but putting out runners and springing up, more luxuriantly, in the garden of your neighbour (often a rival vendor). But it's just as possible that its name alone is behind this slander – in Arabic, *tarchun* (tarragon) rhymes with the verb *jachun* (to betray).

Tomatoes: *My tomatoes have rouged their cheeks and gone to show themselves off!*

Truffles: *Brown daughters of the steppe!*
The Hawran Plateau south of Damascus is known for the relatively light-coloured summer truffles that grow there. Depending on how good the crop has been in any particular year, you can find lots of them for sale at the right season.

Watermelons: *Lovely red melon – I'll only sell you it cut in segments!*
This cry indicates that the vendor is so sure his melons are red and sweet that he's happy to cut them open in front of you. Customers only part with their cash once they've had a chance to cast a critical eye on the melon's flesh. These melons generally cost a bit more, but at least you're sure of getting a properly ripe, sweet one. If, on cutting the fruit open, the vendor finds a greenish-white, unripe melon, he chucks it away and takes the hit.
or: *A dessert for you, a snack for the evening, and some fodder for your donkey!*
An accurate thumbnail sketch of the watermelon. Its sweet red flesh is for dessert, while the lightly toasted seeds are a favourite snack, and the green

skin, which always has plenty of bits of sweet flesh still clinging to it, is popular as fodder for donkeys, horses and sheep.

Nadia, or
Of a neighbour and her fish

Whenever Marie felt like some fish, her favourite place to eat was at her neighbour Nadia's. Nadia, a widow, lived three doors away and specialised in dishes involving fish and seafood, because she came originally from the Lebanon. I also learnt some handy tips from her about how to tell whether fish is fresh: the eyes must be prominent, clear and free of any milkiness. It shouldn't have too pungent a smell. The fins should be firm and the gills bright red. One final fail-safe was the ubiquitous Mediterranean 'nosy finger' technique: pressing down lightly on the belly with your index finger will easily tell you whether a fish is fresh or not. If it is, the small depression you've made will quickly plump out again and revert to its original shape.

Nadia's fish dishes tasted better than all her neighbours'. Whether grilled, boiled or baked, they were without exception nothing short of delicious.

Even so, the real stars of the show were her tuna fish salad and a spicy dish she made with prawns.

Almost for want of anything better, it's not uncommon for restaurants to have a tuna fish salad on their menu in which the tuna seems little more than an embarrassing afterthought. By contrast, the tuna's the main event in this recipe. Nadia also sometimes comes up with some brilliant ways of presenting her dishes, which give those who enjoy that kind of thing as much pleasure as the dishes themselves. Others, though, prefer the food to speak for itself and regard all presentation as unnecessary frippery.

So, on one occasion, Nadia decorated the table by putting tiny mussel shells between the place settings, not so obtrusively that they got in the way of anyone eating but still created a lovely Mediterranean atmosphere. Also, she once served her tuna fish salad in scooped-out orange halves. After slicing the oranges in half, she had carefully eased the flesh away from the peel with a sharp knife, leaving neat little bowls that she filled with the salad before arranging them on a plain, dark-glazed serving dish. She saved the flesh for dessert, as there's nothing better after a fish main course than a fruit salad with lots of citrus in it. It both freshens your breath and aids your digestion.

❋ سلطة سمك الطون ❋
Tuna fish salad

Serves 4 people
400 g canned tuna steak
200 g small cocktail tomatoes
1 clove of garlic
100 green olives (stoned)
1 red pepper
1 onion
1 tsp freshly ground coriander
1 small bunch of parsley
1 lemon
salt and pepper

It's essential that you choose the best quality tuna for this dish – firm fillets packed in pure oil. Cheap, mushy tinned tuna is completely lacking in taste.

Empty the contents of the can into a large mixing bowl. Wash and dry the red pepper and onion, chop them into small pieces and add to the tuna. After carefully rinsing the parsley, chop finely and add to the mix, along with the olives, salt, pepper, ground coriander, oil and lemon juice. Squeeze the garlic clove over the mixture through a garlic press and stir in. Wash the tomatoes, cut them into quarters, sprinkle over the finished salad, and serve immediately.

Best eaten with warm white bread (a baguette or some Turkish pide) and a glass of white wine.

✱ (جمبري حريف) قريدس حرّ ✱
Spicy prawns

1 kg large prawns
3 spring onions or shallots
2 large red peppers
2 unwaxed lemons
5 cloves garlic
20 g fresh ginger root
50 ml olive oil
2 tbsp tomato purée
salt

First rinse the red peppers, discarding the stem and seeds, and cut into small, thin strips no longer than 3 centimetres long by 3 millimetres wide. Chop the roots and most of the green tops off the spring onions (they should be the slim sort, no thicker than 1 cm) so that you're just left with the white and pale green parts. Wash and cut into small rounds.

Peel the prawns, taking care to get rid of every last bit of shell, then rinse and dry them.

Now prepare the spicy infusion for the prawns. In a saucepan, bring 1 litre of water to the boil; in a bowl, combine the sliced red peppers, the five peeled whole garlic cloves, the juice of 1 lemon and the fresh ginger root, finely diced. Add this mix to the boiling water and cook for about 2 to 3 minutes before

*adding the peeled prawns and simmering for a further 3
minutes.*

Lift the prawns out of the broth and discard the rest.

*Meanwhile, prepare a sauce by putting the olive oil, tomato
purée and the juice of the remaining lemon into a large serving
bowl with the chopped spring onions (or shallots). Mix the
ingredients thoroughly before adding the prawns and stirring
them a couple of times to coat them with the sauce. As before,
white bread and white wine are the ideal accompaniments.*

There's all manner of exotic cuisine to be had in Damascus these days. But
where fish is concerned, the golden rule will always be: the simpler, the
better:

Baked whole fish
The simplest way of preparing fish

*1 large (1–2 kg) sea bass, or wild salmon (cleaned and gutted,
but not filleted)*
1 tbsp salt
1 teaspoon ground black pepper
1tbsp ground coriander
1tbsp oregano
2 unwaxed lemons
3 cloves garlic
3 tbsp olive oil

For the sauce:
200 g tahini (sesame seed paste)
1 large lemon
1 clove garlic
1 tbsp salt
Small bunch of parsley

Wash the fish and pat it dry with some kitchen paper. Rub it with the salt inside and out. In a dish, stir together the crushed garlic cloves, the juice of one of the lemons, olive oil, oregano, and the ground pepper and coriander. Now rub this marinade all over the outside of the fish; if there's any left over, rub it into the body cavity. Take the second lemon and cut it into thin slices; do the same with the squeezed-out halves of the first lemon, and press the whole lot into the body cavity. Finally, drizzle some olive oil over the fish and rub it in thoroughly, and pour the remainder into an ovenproof baking tin or earthenware dish (choose one with high sides to avoid spillages, and large enough to lay the fish flat in). Place the marinaded fish in the dish and bake for 40 minutes at 200°C (400°F).

Serve piping hot, straight out of the oven. Choose whatever accompaniment you like: rice, sauté potatoes, chips, or jacket-baked potatoes all go well. And, of course – indispensable with fish – a nice mixed salad.

The tahini sauce is a universal accompaniment to all kinds of fish dishes in Damascus. Here's how to prepare it:

❊ صلصة طرطور ❊

Tahini sauce
(Tarator)

This sesame paste crops up in several recipes, such as Tis'iyye (Spicy Bread–Chickpea Soup; p.97); Aubergine Purée; p.113); and Hummus (p. 181)

It goes by various names: Arab grocers call it Tahine, while the Turks refer to it as Tahin. Ground sesame-seed paste is a very thick, nutritious, brownish-grey coloured gloop (not to be confused withh sesame oil).

To make up the tarator, first mix the tahini with the lemon

*juice before adding 1 tablespoon of salt and a dribble of water.
Stir this vigorously with a spoon until it emulsifies into a pale-
coloured, runny sauce about the same consistency as yoghurt.
Mix in a crushed clove of garlic and some chopped parsley.*

*Some people in Damascus like this sauce so much that they use
it as a dip for all sorts of different food.*

✳ سمك السلمون مع خضار ✳

Fillet of salmon served on a bed of vegetables

Serves 4–6 people
6 salmon fillets
2 onions
1 clove garlic
1 small bunch of parsley
1 kg fresh tomatoes
1 large lemon
200 ml water
100 ml olive oil
1 tbsp salt
1 tsp ground black pepper
1 tbsp ground coriander
1 tsp ground paprika (mild)
1 tsp hot ground paprika

*Peel the onions, chop them roughly and fry them in the olive
oil over a moderate heat until soft. Wash the tomatoes and
dice finely. Add some finely chopped garlic to the onion and fry
for a minute or so. Wash finely chopped leaves of parsley and
put them, together with the tomatoes, into the frying pan. Stir
gently, adding the lemon juice, salt and other spices. Leave to
bubble away gently for about 15 minutes.*

*Once cooked, spoon out half of the fried vegetable mix into an
ovenproof glass or ceramic casserole dish. Lay the fillets of fish on*

top and top with the remainder of the mixture, making sure all the fish is covered. Bake in a preheated oven at 200°C (400°F) for 15–20 minutes.

No need to restrict yourself to the vegetables mentioned in this recipe. Experiment with roughly chopped red peppers, potatoes, carrots, leeks, or courgettes – whatever takes your fancy.

Again, rice or chips as an accompaniment, as you like – but whatever you do, don't forget the salad.
Goes best with a chilled, dry white wine.

❊ حساء سمك ❊
Mediterranean fish soup

The real glory of this soup is its colourful mix of ingredients – a delight for the eye and the taste buds alike. It'd be spoilt by making it too fiery, so go easy on the spices.

800 g fish fillets (a mix of 4 or 5 different fish – say, salmon, redfish (or red bream), pike-perch, or cod. Monkfish and hake would also work fine)
200 g prawn tails
200 ml dry white wine
2 large onions
2 carrots
200 g celery
1 small bulb of fennel
1 red pepper
300 g tomatoes
2 garlic cloves
100 ml olive oil
1 tbsp salt
1 tsp ground black pepper
1 tbsp oregano
A few fresh basil leaves

Roughtly chop the onions and the other vegetables and sweat for a few minutes in the olive oil. Add chopped garlic and white wine and leave to simmer for a short while, until the vegetables are cooked through but still have some bite to them. Add a little water to loosen up the mix and bring to a simmer. Meanwhile, rinse the fish fillets, pat dry and cut into large chunks. Add the fish to the soup, but immediately remove the pan from the heat. Leave the fish to steep and cook through in the hot broth for 10 minutes. Season to taste and ladle into soup bowls.

Before serving, the soup can be garnished with chopped tomato and fresh basil leaves.

Makes a meal in itself with a crusty baguette and a glass of chilled white wine.

❋ فطائر سمك السلمون ❋
Salmon pastry parcels

Serves 4–6 people
250 g filo pastry (deep frozen)
500 g salmon fillet (fresh or frozen).
2 tbsp sunflower oil
2 tbsp butter
2 tbsp chopped parsley
1tsp ground black pepper
1tsp salt
1 egg
1 lemon

Thaw the sheets of filo and cut into squares, no smaller than 5 × 5 centimetres and no larger than 10 × 10. Let them rest for a few minutes on a non-stick baking sheet.

Preheat the oven to 200°C (400°F).

Put the sunflower oil into a frying pan and warm over a

moderate heat. Add the buttter and let it melt before adding chunks of salmon fillet (cut into cubes roughly 2 × 2 cm) and frying them lightly. Finish off with the lemon juice, parsley, salt and pepper, cover the pan and simmer gently for 5 minutes.

Allow the fish to cool down slightly, then spoon a little into the middle of each pastry square. Moisten the edges of the squares with a wetted finger or a pastry brush, and pull up the four corners to the centre to make a little parcel, pressing together firmly to ensure that the edges stick. Your finished parcels should look like small pastry envelopes. Beat the egg and carefully brush over each parcel.

Bake for 10 minutes until nicely browned.

Serve with a mixed salad and white wine.

✳ الأرز مع قريدس وخضار ✳
Pilaf with prawns

Serves 4–6 people

500 g prawns

500 g long-grain rice

2 tbsp butter

2 tbsp olive oil

2 large onions

1 red pepper

1 green pepper

200 g green peas or petit pois (fresh or frozen, but never the tinned variety)

1 carrot

1tsp ground green peppercorns

1tsp salt

1tsp ground coriander

2tbsp pine kernels

Pour the olive oil into a frying pan and place over moderate heat until hot. Add the butter and stir until it melts.

Peel the carrots and dice finely. Skin the onions, de-seed the peppers and remove their stalks, rinse and cut into 1cm squares. Add the pine kernels to the pan, and continue cooking for 5 minutes.

Wash the prawns and green peas, pat dry and add to the pan, along with the pepper, coriander and salt. Fry at a low heat for 2 minutes.

Now add the rice, mixing well, and pour in enough water to ensure that it covers the rice to a depth of 1 cm. Bring quickly to the boil, then reduce the heat to the lowest setting and simmer for around 30 minutes, until the rice has absorbed all the liquid. (Whatever you do, don't stir it!!!)

Serve the prawn pilaf with a salad, and a glass of red or white wine, as you like.

Abu Bashir, or
Of generosity, hospitality and other rarities

Once you have reached the Bab Touma Gate, which gives the entire Christian Quarter its name, and are standing with your back to the Old City, you can see the beginning of the new city and the elegant, modern Christian area Kassa', where several of my girlfriends and relatives live. Actually, they originally came from the Old City and most still have siblings here. That is where I will visit them, because if I attempted to describe all of Damascus we would get lost. No, I would rather stay in the Old City, which still has so many stories to offer and so many artists of the kitchen whose secrets I want to share with you.

But before we turn around and walk back to Straight Street to continue our stroll through the Old City, I have to mention someone who carried on his business not far from here, just outside the walls. Do you remember old Abu Bashir who had a little restaurant on the right, not far from the Gate, and who offered only one dish day and night, namely Ful, boiled broad beans?

When Abu Bashir died, the city lost a piece of typically Damascene generosity, such as used to be quite normal. If you try to tell his story to young people and children nowadays, they think you are making it up. But Abu Bashir's restaurant existed into the early 1970s. Two queues began to form at his door in the early morning. One queue was of people patiently waiting for a table. The other was a bunch of children standing there with bowls in hand waiting to get their boiled beans. The Damascenes enjoyed this hearty, inexpensive breakfast.

Ful, the broad bean, also known as fava bean, horse bean, butter bean, Windsor bean or English bean, is an ancient plant from the Mediterranean. The Egyptians, Romans, Greeks and Hebrews knew it as a foodstuff as early as 1,000 BC. It continues to flourish in numerous varieties. It is cheap and very nourishing. Today, however, the broad bean is becoming more and more a sign of poverty. Snide sayings and silly jokes warn people against enjoying them because they supposedly make you stupid, which is rubbish of course. Only someone who has come into money and does not want to be reminded of his past would say such a thing.

One thing is certain, however: this bean is an energy capsule. Unfortunately, depending on how sensitive your stomach is, it can also be very difficult to digest. In addition, it is laborious and time consuming to prepare, which is why Damascenes only rarely cook broad beans at home any more. Instead, they prefer to collect their beans from the small restaurants that cook them in vast quantities overnight and are sold out by midday, day after day. Nowadays the dish is called Ful Medames. *Medames* means 'buried in hot ash', one of the oldest, most environmentally friendly and certainly most flavourful methods of cooking.

In the old days the restaurants would bring tightly sealed, heat resistant clay containers (they looked like huge jugs) filled with beans and water to the hammams in their area every evening. The stokers would bury the jugs deep in the hot ash and keep shovelling more hot ash on them all night because the fire under the great boiler of a hammam blazes for almost 20 hours a day.

The stoker would be given a few piasters for each jug, which helped to top up his meagre income, and for the restaurants it was incredibly convenient and economical. Early in the morning they would collect their jugs, which the boiler man had cleaned of ashes for them. Beans cooked in this kind of slow heat taste the best.

Abu Bashir always took his many jugs to be buried in the ashes at Hammam Bakri, which we mentioned earlier. He is supposed to have sworn as a young man that no guest would every leave his restaurant hungry. Every customer received a large plateful of wonderful smelling beans and ate and drank hot, sweet tea, tightly squeezed in amongst the other customers and tables. If you finished your food, but were still not yet full, you could take your plate back up to the counter and say *'Sallih'*, which means something like improve, correct, repair. You would then receive a complimentary second portion, somewhat smaller than the first portion, but every bit as freshly seasoned. If necessary, Abu Bashir would dish out a second 'repair'. Not even a hippopotamus could consume a third one.

When Abu Bashir died, his son dispensed with the commercially damaging custom of refilling plates for nothing, and soon moved to the Salihiyya Quarter of the modern city. He owns a restaurant there, one that is not much different from hundreds of others. No one confused Abu Bashir for any other. I know of neighbours who used to go from the Abbara all the way to Abu Bashir, bypassing ten other Ful restaurants along the way, just to breakfast in his.

Ful
Boiled Broad Beans with Piquant Sauce

250 g dried small broad beans
1 small onion or shallot
2 lemons
1 small bunch flat leafed parsley
2 ripe, but firm tomatoes
1 garlic clove
1 tsp salt
½ tsp cumin
Coarsely ground pepper
100 ml olive oil

Wash the beans, removing any small stones. Soak overnight in 2 l water. The next morning bring to the boil and then simmer for 2 hours over lowest heat.

While this is happening, prepare the other ingredients. Peel, finely dice and set aside the onion. Squeeze the lemon juice. Remove stalks from the parsley, wash and finely chop. Wash, de-seed and finely chop the tomatoes. Place in a bowl.

When the beans are cooked (the skin may have a bit of bite, but the core should be soft), remove with a ladle, drain and place in a large bowl. Add the crushed garlic, lemon juice and salt. Mix carefully. Add the parsley and tomatoes. Season with a pinch of cumin and pepper and drizzle with the olive oil.

Crispy white bread and hot black tea goes well with this dish.

Having reminisced about Abu Bashir, let us turn around. We will reach Straight Street at the Kishle junction in about 10 minutes. That is where we started our jaunt to Bab Touma.

Over the course of centuries, Straight Street has collected several additional labels, all of which survive to this day. One of these is Medhat Pasha Street, but it never applied to the entire length of the street. Other names refer to very specific sections of the street. The boundaries where one stops and another starts have never really been pinned down, like so many things in Damascus. At any rate, east of the junction, Straight Street is called Bab Sharqi Street; 100 metres to the west of the crossing, where the Roman Arch stands, I am absolutely certain it is called Medhat Pasha Street. The area around the Roman Arch is also called the 'Quarter of Ancient Ruins'. All of these sections of road are also just part of 'Straight Street'.

If we now continue our stroll from the Kishle junction to the west along Straight Street, we come to a tiny alley that is not even two metres wide, called *Juwaniyye*, 'inner'. Narrow and shady, it snakes through an area of buildings that appears humble from the outside but actually includes some of the loveliest flats available. If you take the right turn at every fork in the alley, you will eventually end up back on Bab Touma Street. If you keep to the left, you come back to Straight Street.

Cousin Takla lives with her husband Ramsi just before the alley opens onto to Straight Street. Ramsi was still a schoolboy when he met Takla for the first time. He immediately fell in love and used every opportunity to see her. He was three years older than her brother, but befriended the spoiled, tiresome boy nevertheless, to be around Takla as much as possible. Takla reciprocated his affection and gave him high marks for putting up with the little 'hippo' that everyone in the Quarter referred to as the walking stomach. The boy was as broad as he was tall. Both of them took advantage of the fact that he didn't notice anything, so long as you kept feeding him.

Ramsi lived four houses away from Takla. One day they discovered a path across the flat rooftops. If he could muster the courage to cover a short difficult stretch by balancing his way across a courtyard, they would be able to meet unnoticed on the roof at night. This was Takla's greatest wish and Ramsi wanted nothing more than to grant his beloved her desire. Ramsi did his balancing act.

Night after night he would tread carefully along a narrow, four-metrelong beam until he safely reached the roof on the other side. Takla and Ramsi considered themselves the bravest lovers in Arab history, because there was as yet no one in literature who balanced his way to his beloved high up on a beam.

But life is not literature. One night a neighbour, who had come out to go to the toilet, found a man above her head under the open sky balancing on a narrow beam. She thought he was a thief and screamed. The boy was frightened to death. He lost his balance. But there was a silver lining: he was able to cling to the beam. He begged the woman to be quiet, but that only made her more hysterical and she screamed until all the neighbours had woken up and someone had called the police.

Ramsi lied to protect Takla. He claimed he wanted to break into the flat of an engineer who was away on holiday and steal his record collection. The police thought this young man who was willing to risk his life for a few silly albums was not quite right in the head. Ramsi was released, but from then on labelled crazy, but Takla remained true to him. She refused all men and told her kind-hearted parents she wanted only him. When the parents could no longer see any other alternative, they approved her marriage to the lunatic Ramsi.

Their wedding was celebrated, and, as her husband was practically destitute, the young couple were given two rooms in Takla's parents' house. The little house is sweet, but a cough echoes into every last nook and cranny. So the two had to live a quiet life from then on, which is not healthy for a loving relationship.

After exactly three years and two children they were bored to death. If you visit them today, you have to take care you are not infected by their boredom. Although Takla is an excellent cook, I don't like to go there. Good hospitality is more than good cooking; a good host offers magical nourishment for the brain, and the heart, as well. Takla and Ramsi are not gifted in this department. Sometimes, though, when she phones me with some important news, I go to see her. One such was the time when she was hopeful that her brother, who had been living in exile in France for 15 years, might be granted amnesty.

Through various connections and all sorts of bribes an important general was persuaded to come to dinner and hear her brother's story. There was a chance they could persuade him to intervene on the man's behalf. The family was gripped by nervous excitement.

Takla's greatest culinary achievement is a classic lamb dish. Real lamb should be very tender: problems only arise if the lamb is in fact a toothless old ram, which the butcher has called lamb out of pure affection. Then the meal will have a strong odour and you will need all your skill to conceal the smell and make the food edible.

The house was trembling with anxiety. I could feel it as soon as I walked in. The old mother and the practically blind father were pacing up and down in the little courtyard. They wanted to hide because they were afraid they would make a poor impression on the general. I asked them to stay because they looked so distraught – after all, the general, who was not even forty years old, also had parents. Maybe their misery would move him more than the meal and he would put in a good word for the disgraced boy for the sake of the parents. Takla smoked one cigarette after the other. I asked her to stop smoking and open a window so that the meat would not also taste of smoke. Then I made her a strong mocha and sat her down in the corner. She was not to move, just say what needed doing and I would do exactly as she said, being hellishly careful not to add a grain too much salt to the meal. It all worked out beautifully.

❈ لحم خروف بالفرن ❈
Baked Lamb

Only the best meat is good enough for this delectable dish. Filet of lamb, or another good cut, will taste wonderful.

500 g lean lamb
2 large onions
500 g tomatoes, skinned
4 tbsp olive oil
¼ l red wine
4 large garlic cloves
1 tsp salt
1 tsp pepper
1 tsp rosemary
1 tsp thyme

Wash, pat dry and dice the meat into small cubes. Peel the onions and chop finely. Cut the tomatoes into small dice. (For this dish you can also used tinned tomatoes and cut them into small pieces.) Heat the oil in a large frying pan, stir in the meat and brown for about 5 minutes. Add the wine, onions, peeled and crushed garlic, salt, pepper, rosemary and thyme and mix thoroughly. Put everything into a heatproof dish, cover and bake in an oven preheated to 220° C/425° F/Gas Mark 7 for an hour. Uncover and bake for another 15 minutes.

Rice and green beans are superb with this dish.

❈ *If the meat begins to dry out, add ¼ l wine. If it is too watery, leave it to cook in the oven for another 15 minutes at*

150° C/300° F/Gas Mark 2; but please do not add any flour or starch.

At the end, Takla said: 'Naturally you could leave the lamb to marinate in a litre of red wine overnight in the refrigerator and then work with it the next day. That's what the best cooks do. The dish takes on more of a wine flavour then.' You would then skip the browning step, but the olive oil would still need to be added to the seasoning mixture.

We cooked for hours, drank lots of coffee and together tried to work out how Takla should broach the subject. Perhaps it would be best to wait until the general commented on the meal. I was certain he would like it. Takla makes this dish maybe twenty times a year and her guests have always been enthusiastic – none more so than I. Even Muhammad, the family's Muslim neighbour, always wants this dish. When Takla, more out of politeness than serious concern, points out that the lamb has been bathing in alcohol all night, that pious but humorous man dismisses her worries: 'There is no alcohol left at 250° C (475° F/Gas Mark 9). Islam forbids the consumption of alcohol, not its existence. It is no reasonable person's business what the lamb gets up to on the way to the oven.'

We rehearsed the conversation over and over. I could have cried for sympathy at how Takla, who loved her brother, trembled and yet tried to appear calm.

'Does he require gifts?' The question suddenly burst from my mouth.

'No, he is decent and does not demand anything. But the path to him cost us a lot of money. Even his chauffeur took a cut.'

The general had wanted to eat at noon. The table was set just before twelve. I went home and waited by the phone.

It rang around four o'clock.

I could barely make out what Takla was saying at the other end of the line. The general had had someone ring at three o'clock to say he would not be able to come that day but he would turn up the following week. Takla knew the general would never come and that the whole thing had been a swindle.

And she was right.

If you turn left from Takla's house, you are quickly back on Straight Street. If you continue on a few steps towards the Roman Arch, you reach the house of Aunt Sahar, a distant cousin of my mother's. She lives there with a miser. There are not many tightwads of his calibre on this earth: if there were, the world would have been long since doomed. But Aunt Sahar and her husband have a special chapter of their own.

The ruse, or
Of misers and sus sellers

Miserliness is an evil illness. Thank God that it is not infectious, that, indeed, it is quite the opposite: most who come into contact with a miser become immune to the disease, since those who live near someone infected by the meanness bug discover just how wretchedly it can ruin people.

Tight-fisted people may not stand out as much in other cultures, but in Damascus, where hospitality practically counts as one of the holy commandments, meanness is a public sin.

Aunt Sahar married her husband Antun more by accident than anything else. His parents rented a house that belonged to her father and Antun used to come to Aunt Sahar's to pay the rent. He was polite and proper. It was said of him that he would achieve something because he worked hard and was not wasteful. Aunt Sahar, in contrast, was always a spendthrift, as well as being chaotic, funny and something of a dreamer.

When she was about seventeen, she fell in love with a Lebanese seaman who was in Damascus for a short time. They wanted to marry and emigrate to America, but one day the sailor did not turn up to the agreed meeting place. Rumours spread that he had a lover in every city, and that a mulatta in Colombia had poisoned him out of jealousy. Others claimed he had fallen overboard on a stormy night and lay buried under the foamy waves. In any event, Aunt Sahar locked her love for the seaman away behind three doors in the deepest chamber of her heart and got on with her life.

She was bored to tears in the quiet of her parents' house. When Antun inquired by way of his mother, one year after the sailor's disappearance, whether she would marry him, she said yes. It was a purely pragmatic decision: she thought she could carry on a marriage with Antun that would never touch the love behind the doors in her heart.

Antun quickly grasped how to make a lot of money in Damascus: import/export. He obtained the right to do business for a globally known automobile company and soon had branches in Homs, Hama and Aleppo in addition to his main office in Damascus. He became rich, super rich. But as his wallet grew, his soul shrank into a tiny, hard lump of miserliness.

Aunt Sahar soon realised she could not deal with Antun in a normal manner. Year on year he retreated deeper and deeper into his strange labyrinth of frugality. All of a sudden his wife had to keep meticulous household accounts in which she was to track every penny she spent. So she wrote all sorts of things into the book – except what she actually spent. Antun would review the accounts and be satisfied – though she still had to listen to his usual wails whenever money took its leave of him. Aunt Sahar camouflaged coffee, sugar, pralines, cinema tickets, sweets, gifts, perfume and other luxuries as coal, flour, cleaning materials and heating oil. Antun could not have checked these even if he had wanted to. He was far too busy and on the road for days at a time, managing his businesses.

When he returned home, he would look over the housekeeping book, check the sums, and complain about the amounts and the high consumption of flour, oil and textiles. And Aunt Sahar would explain to him that four growing children need many things and that prices were rising daily.

All four children, two girls and two boys, were sworn accomplices and helped to back up Aunt Sahar's story. Over and over they would annoy their father with demands for new clothes, school supplies and books – which chorus served to dispel any doubts he might have. Consequently, Antun was secretly happy that Aunt Sahar was doing such a wonderful job raising the children. He was equally satisfied that she saved money in her dealings with tradesmen. In fact, she entered large sums for repairs (their house was so old that many repairs were required) to cover her actual outgoings and then had the work done by friendly neighbours or workmen, whom she had to pay little or nothing. The figures she put in her accounts were what she needed for her generous parties.

It is difficult to believe, but Antun was such a skinflint that he would deduct the smallest amounts from his wife's allowance the following month if she made an error in her calculations. That is probably why all four children became maths geniuses. As one of her daughters told me, Aunt Sahar would sometimes intentionally put in errors just so Antun could discover them and be so happy that he would overlook the larger expenditures and provide the necessary money.

Resistance has a thousand and one faces.

As soon as Antun left on one of his business trips, Aunt Sahar would invite us all over, friends and relatives, for a party of sensual pleasures. These days with her children and guests she transformed into a real-life version of the Arabian Nights, and yet, by the time her husband returned, all traces had been so thoroughly removed that not even a police dog could have found the remotest clue. Sahar knew her Antun. We, the guests, would help polish and wash before we left the house.

When Antun returned home, he would be welcomed back with his favourite meal: lentil soup with as few herbs and as little olive oil as possible.

The children would greet him quietly, politely and almost awkwardly. When he carelessly dropped in questions about the events of the day, while spooning his soup into his mouth, they would give him such well-behaved but masterfully crafted answers that any father would have been moved to tears. The four children were not only highly intelligent, they were also little imps when it came to dancing and laughing. That is why they idolised their mother.

Then one day Antun fell seriously ill. Aunt Sahar called the best doctors to his bedside and lied to him when he asked about their fees. It was an unusual illness that consumed him from the inside. For the longest time the doctors thought he was suffering from muscular dystrophy, but that was not it. Aunt Sahar cared for her Antun patiently and lovingly for three years. He died in the autumn of 1970.

She sold her husband's company for good money because none of the children wanted any part of it. Then she bought the beautiful house next door, where she still lives, relieved of any financial worries.

Aunt Sahar is a master cook: she cooks rice in particular better than anyone. In her hands, rice is no tasteless mass, degraded into a neutral space-filler, an anonymous side dish, but instead is transformed into a wide range of enjoyable meals.

❋ ارز المفلفل ❋

Classic Damascene Rice

1 cup fine soup noodles (eg vermicelli)
2 tbsp butterfat
500 g long grain rice
1 tsp salt
1 tsp freshly ground pepper
100 g pine nuts (or 100 g slivered almonds)

Brown the noodles while stirring in the butterfat, then add the rice and fry a further 2 minutes. Add salt and pepper and enough water to clear the rice by 2 cm. Bring to the boil and then let cook for 25 minutes over lowest heat. Do not stir under any circumstances!

When the rice is ready to serve, brown the pine nuts in 1 tbsp of butterfat and sprinkle over.

This is a good side dish for vegetarian, meat or fish entrées. You can also serve the rice as a main course, and accompany it with a light salad, yoghurt and other sauces.

❋ Instead of butterfat, you can also use a mixture of 2 tbsp sunflower oil and 1 tbsp butter. Warm the oil and melt the butter in it.

The most common mistakes with this dish are: using the wrong type of rice, using too much water, not cooking it long enough, turning up the heat too high and ... stirring for lack of patience.

٭ أرز مع لوز ولحم ٭

Rice with Almonds, Meat and Raisins

500 g long grain rice
200 g peeled almonds or pine nuts
1 tbsp butterfat
1 large onion
200 g beef mince
100 g raisins
1 tsp cardamom
½ tsp turmeric
1 tsp cinnamon
1 tsp allspice
1 tsp salt

Rinse the rice and cover with water to soak for 20 minutes. Brown the pine nuts or almonds in butterfat, then remove from the fat and set aside. Peel the onion and finely chop. Fry the onion in the same fat. Add the mince and fry another 5 minutes. Turn off the heat and add the almonds, raisins and spices. Mix well.

Add everything to the rice in a saucepan and add sufficient water to clear the mixture by 1 cm. Bring to the boil, then reduce the heat to the lowest level. Let it sit for 20–25 minutes.

Serve with yoghurt or a light mixed salad.

❊ You can peel the almonds yourself. That is when they taste the best. Cover the almonds with boiling water and let sit for 20 minutes. Then rinse with cold water and squeeze the kernel out of the skin with your fingers.

A few steps from Aunt Sahar's house stands the Roman Arch. On the left before the Arch is an alley that leads into a maze of streets. If you always keep to the left you reach two exits to one street, which is called Tal-al-Hijara. It used to be called Jew Alley and it leads, as you know, back to the Kishle crossing and our Abbara Alley.

Can you hear the cries of the sus sellers? Do you remember the wonderful custom associated with this chilled, bittersweet drink? On special occasions, whether sad or happy, people paid for a vat of sus to be distributed to passers-by. When the neighbours heard of it, they would send out their children with little pots or pails. You drank and wished the newborn, newly married or recently returned traveller well, or said a prayer for a speedy recovery for the ill, or for blessings for the dead: 'May God forgive you and your ancestors your sins, oh giver!' or 'God have mercy on your parents, oh giver,' we would say.

The custom has almost died out, but today of all days Sakine's neighbour is providing this drink because his mother died forty days ago. Sakine's daughter just ran out with a little pail, but not before double-checking with her mother exactly what she was to say when the man gave her the refreshing drink.

The neighbour is a Shi'ite. The Shi'ites are one of the small Muslim minorities in the country. The man who surprised us all with the sus today always adored his mother. I knew her. She was very religious and a wonderful hostess, which is becoming more and more rare.

I remember a day about ten years ago when I visited Sakine. I had the day off. We had not seen each other in ages and agreed to meet for coffee early in the morning at her house. At that hour, her husband had already left for his workshop and her children were in school. Sakine had saved the entire morning for our gossip. Two other girlfriends of hers were also coming to join us. All three of us arrived at Sakine's door at the agreed time, at just the same moment, and started to laugh. We stood there howling with such laughter at our punctuality that we were incapable of ringing the doorbell.

Suddenly this old, but hale, lady looked out from a neighbouring house and shouted to us: 'If you can laugh so gaily then I want to laugh with you. Grab Sakine and come to my place.' And then she closed the window again as if such an invitation were a matter of course. We did not know the woman and thought the request was a joke. Sakine heard our laughter, hurried to the door and had to wait a few moments before we could explain that our laughter had almost earned us a breakfast.

'What do you mean almost?' she said seriously. 'Ayshe is already standing at her door.' And she went to the woman who was standing there, beaming with goodness. We followed Sakine and thus came to savour a majestic breakfast.

At the time I witnessed something unusual and did not really understand it. I knew that the family belonged to the Twelver sect of the Shi'as. I also knew that Islam forbids any images of people because it views a portrait as an act of creation and creation is only allowed to God. In Islam, the imitation of creation borders on blasphemy. Instead the Arabs were, and are, fantastic storytellers – they paint pictures with words. They never got very far with a brush or chisel. If you compare pre-Islamic figures to those of the Greeks and Romans, you will realise clearly enough that the Arabs would never have achieved much in painting even if it had not been forbidden.

It is all because of the desert. It and it alone played midwife to the art of storytelling, while ensuring that the art of painting never grew. What would a Bedouin have painted – yellow on yellow on ochre on brown on yellow on yellow-brown? The desert does not provide much stimulus for the eye; rather, it forces the tongue to speak so that you are not suffocated by loneliness.

The Persians were different. They excelled at painting miniatures and continue to do so to this day, despite Islam. Only with God, Muhammad and the angels do they make compromises, leaving the face white or veiled.

In any event, it was the first time in my life that I saw a Shi'ite home from the inside. On almost every wall of the house hung pictures of an aloofly beautiful man with a halo almost like Christ's and a curious sword in his hand.

'Who's that?' I asked quietly.

'Ali,' whispered Sakine. 'They view him as a saint,' she added. Later I saw the same picture, which apparently came from Persia, on a poster in a small bookstore owned by a Shi'ite.

Tis'iyye, also called *Tisqiyee*, was the old lady's speciality. The name means soaked. I have eaten this dish many times, but will always remember Ayshe's version as the tastiest. I was at her place two or three times over the following years and each time I asked for this dish. One time I asked if I could give her a hand so I could watch while she cooked it. The old lady laughed merrily. Later I wrote it all down.

❋ تسقية ❋

Tis'iyye
Spicy Bread-Chickpea Soup

200 g dried chickpeas
1 large baguette
5 garlic cloves
500 g yoghurt
2 tbsp vinegar or lemon juice
2 tsp salt
1 tsp pepper
50 g pine nuts
100 g butterfat
1 small bunch parsley
2 tsp ground cumin

Wash the chickpeas and allow to soak over-night. Cook until soft in ample water, about 1 to 1 ½ hours.

Cut the bread into small cubes and toast to golden brown in the oven. Peel the garlic and crush it with a bit of salt. Add half the garlic to the cooking chickpeas and the other half to the yoghurt. Add the vinegar or lemon juice, salt and pepper to the yoghurt and mix well.

Brown (not blacken) the pine nuts in butterfat and keep warm in the fat.

Wash and finely chop the parsley.

Warm a porcelain or heat-resistant glass bowl in the oven.

The final part of the preparation is quick and the food must then be served right away, so only start the next steps once the guests are seated at the table.

Remove the bowl from the oven and put the bread in it. Lift the chickpeas out of their broth, allow to drain, and then spread on the bread. The layer of bread and chickpeas should not be thicker than 10 cm. That is what needs to guide the choice of serving bowl.

Bring the remaining chickpea broth to a boil and carefully ladle the hot broth over the bread until it is all well soaked, but do not use too much broth, or it will all go soupy. Distribute the yoghurt-vinegar mixture evenly and smooth it out with a large spoon. Sprinkle on the cumin and the parsley. Then add the pine nuts including the butterfat and serve immediately.

In Damascus we drink hot tea with this.

❧ You can also prepare the chickpeas in another way. Mash them to a purée together with tahini, lemon and garlic, as you would when making hummus (see page 181), then thin this mash with a bit of the broth until it has the consistency of yoghurt. Pour this over the soaked bread and smooth it out. Skip the yoghurt and vinegar, as the mash already has a bit of an acidic taste from the lemon, then continue on with the recipe as described above.

Sometimes it is advisable to wait and brown the pine nuts at the very end and sprinkle them on the yoghurt while still hot. But you need two people to do this, so that one can be frying the pine nuts, while the other is carrying out the final stages of the recipe.

The Mirage, or
Of ice manufacturers and professional mourners

Let's return to Straight Street in order to disappear from there again and dive into the confusion of the alleys. If you are standing at the restored Roman Arch and look back toward the east, you will see on the left side – set back a bit – the largest orthodox church: the Miryamiyya or St Mary's Church. This is where the Patriarch of the Greek-Orthodox Christians resides. The church has a turbulent past. It was built prior to the Arab conquest. The Arab victors generally tolerated its existence, but it was repeatedly destroyed when the Muslims were having a difficult time and the Christians were meant to have an even more difficult time. The accusation was always the same: treason, collaboration with the enemy. In times of crisis, the majority of a society rarely has any better ideas. The angry mob burnt the church down in 1260, 1400 and 1860.

But hope for the future and the determination to work for this future gave the congregants of the orthodox minority the strength to rebuild the church anew each time.

I probably do not need to help you recall any of this history. I would rather remind you of something else that also has to do with St Mary's Church, something to laugh about. Do you remember the strange feeling we would always have at Easter? Our Catholic church follows the western (Gregorian) calendar while the Orthodox Church follows the eastern (Julian). Just when Jesus had left his grave and was hurrying toward heaven, He was being crucified again 200 metres down the road.

The Orthodox Church was veiling itself in their black mourning robes on their Good Friday while we Catholics fancied Jesus was already safely with his Heavenly Father. The calendar bureaucrats could not have made themselves appear more absurd.

An alley leads from Straight Street, past the church into a labyrinth of relatively quiet alleys. Again and again there are houses here that exude modesty from the outside but provide a paradise for the eyes on the inside. We will come to speak of some of these houses, which we will encounter on our way to the centre of the Old City – the Umayyad Mosque. In order to get there you have to turn left behind St Mary's Church, onto a street that runs parallel to Straight Street. Elias, our Uncle Butros' brother-in-law, lives just past the first alley that leads back to Straight Street.

Elias is a mathematician. When he was still young, he fell so deeply in love with his colleague, Shadya, that he was willing to risk his life for her. Her parents, farmers from the conservative south, did not accept the townsman. But sometimes fortune smiles so that life remains worth living. After initially fierce resistance, Elias and Shadya were allowed to live together. Their luck seemed complete.

Yet anyone who would see them now, after 20 years of marriage, would think they were siblings. They are polite and proper to each other but there seems to be no spark of love, not even warmth. The fire of passion seems to have gone out. Shadya has become a thoughtful, quiet woman who is almost stiff with restraint. She teaches geography and history and is well read, but she appears as mute as a Sphinx, unwilling to reveal what she knows.

Elias, on the other hand, is talkative and frequently ironical or even sarcastic. He is always good for intelligent entertainment, but I cannot help thinking he talks so much in order to distract from his pain. His irony is a mask behind which he hides his disappointments.

Shadya never cooks. No one knows why. She has no connection to cooking and would happily live on spaghetti with tomato sauce for weeks.

By contrast, Elias was once a gourmet and an excellent cook as well, but unfortunately he has lost any inclination for cooking, as Shadya does not care what is put on the table as long as there is something. There could be no worse punishment for a cook.

That is why I have never been to their home for dinner. At most I have visited them for tea, though his wife drank only coffee. Every time I visited she would politely ask what I would like to drink and only there would I answer 'Tea', as a small declaration of support for Elias's cooking ability. Even when he is just preparing tea you can see how much he enjoys cooking. He celebrates it like a religious ceremony. I find his tea extraordinarily delicious, even more so than any conversation with him. Elias studies Damascene customs and folk tales and dreams of writing an encyclopaedia about the customs of Damascus, their origins and development.

I learned a few things from him about the surprisingly complex relations between different customs in the city. Do you hear the call of the turtledove? Yes? Then the heat of the day has begun to let up. Damascenes have always held their siesta during the midday heat. The streets empty between one and three o'clock and for as long as it stays hot the turtledove falls silent. Only when the Damascenes hear the laughing voice of the turtledove, do they begin to come out of their houses again. Elias went on to explain to me why Damascenes have such a close relationship to the turtledove. They love this bird and it is considered a disgrace to kill one – some even consider the turtledove to be holy, as it is supposed to have fluttered around the grave of the Prophet Muhammad, to keep it cool and shaded. Perhaps it is just a superstition, but if a superstition has such sensible consequences, then I am happy to be superstitious.

Now, even the simplest matter has many different facets in Damascus. Tea or coffee is a question of preference, but a rule of thumb has developed over the centuries: a Muslim prefers to drink tea, while a Christian prefers coffee. Why? It is said that this resulted from the poverty of a broad section of the Muslim population. Tea could and still can be obtained inexpensively everywhere here. As a rule, the urban Christians were wealthier and preferred to drink the expensive brew. It was also considered more mannerly to sip coffee from dainty little cups than loudly to slurp tea from glasses. It may have been proven that slurping improves the appreciation of tea's aroma, but it still sounds like the grunts of a snoring man. The Christians, who were copying European manners by the 18th century, had the crazy notion that drinking coffee was more posh.

Coffee has always been considered a luxury good, whereas tea was simply a commodity. Hot tea with bread and sugar fed entire generations of poor people. Strict rulers, by way of contrast, have repeatedly forbidden the enjoyment of coffee. Tea never got a bad reputation for its intoxicating effect, even though it contains more caffeine than coffee – it just takes longer to have an effect.

If you listen to everything I have just told you about coffee and tea, it all sounds so convincing and logical. But in reality, once you have travelled to the Syrian steppes and met the poorest Muslim Bedouin who barely has enough to eat but who serves his guest a heavenly coffee with cardamom, then the theory seems grey and useless.

However that may be, Christians as a rule drink more coffee and Muslims more tea. Do you remember? You were the only one in our family who drank tea several times a day and would only drink coffee when compelled to do so because we had guests. At the time you had gotten the nickname 'our Muslim' from our neighbour, Halil. To this day, every time he sees me on the street, the old man says to me, 'Give our regards to our Muslim. Does he still drink as much tea?' I always answer, as if in a litany, 'He drinks even more. He drinks even more.' And he laughs toothlessly.

Elias uses the best tea varieties: aromatic Darjeeling and robust Assam are his favourites.

He rinses the teapot with hot water, reckoning on about ½ litre water per 10 g of tea and pours boiling water over the tea. Then he lets the tea steep for 3 minutes. Not longer! And then he serves it in prewarmed little tea glasses that are very popular here and much handier than cups, which are only used in elegant homes. Sometimes he puts a fresh mint leaf in the glass before he fills it with tea. The tea then gets a hint of peppermint, which is effective against thirst in the summer. I did not and do not like any additives in my tea and have always requested that my tea be served pure, but you can add as much sugar or milk as you like. Eating a few nuts beforehand also intensifies the flavour of the tea.

Many Damascenes boil the tea with the water. Elias thinks that is bad because much more tannic acid is released and the tea tastes bitter. Incidentally it was also from him that I got the tip never to wash a metal teapot on the inside. The brown layer deposited by the tea prevents the metal from coming into contact with the brew and thus allows the aroma to develop wonderfully.

There is a small flat in Elias and Shadya's house with its own separate entrance. This is where the famous Halime lives, a professional mourner. She lives well from it, because the Damascenes like to show their grief as publicly as as their joy. Loud sobbing in the community helps them to dispel the bitterness of their loss from their hearts. As some fear that people may be inhibited at the funeral of their loved one and will not cry sufficiently loudly, they hire professional mourners, *Nawaha* in Arabic, which sometimes leads to unintended moments of comic relief.

Halime has a lovely voice and a good memory, so she has memorised a number of common formulae that are normally spoken of the dead. She can wail as long as it takes for all the other mourners to begin to sob – that is what she is paid for. It is amazing how a man insufferable in life can practically become a saint in death. Some joke about Halime that she sometimes has so many funerals in one day that she gets her lamentations mixed up. It happened once, that at her fourth or fifth funeral in a row, she was bemoaning the loss of a man, enthusiastically praising his virility and manful acts of bravery, when a woman nudged her in the side and not so gently pointed out that it was a woman lying in the coffin, who even in the best of circumstances could not have been considered virile, even if she was a bit masculine.

My friend Hala used to live a few houses further on. She came from a prosperous family. Her father was the first in Syria to produce ice. Before refrigerators became affordable and every house had electricity, ice was a treasured item, particularly in the summer months. Ice has been a rarity in the Middle East since ancient times. It was brought down from the mountain villages surrounding Damascus and then stored in caves. The village Menin made a particular name for itself in this trade. There were even ships that would bring ice from Syria and the Lebanon to Egypt for a lot of money. It was considered the height of luxury to consume ice-chilled drinks in hot Egypt.

Hala's father, always ahead of his time, opened a small factory that was able to transform water into ice in the flash of an eye. It was a sensation. Many would have paid a fee just to tour the factory – that is how unbelievable what was happening behind the walls appeared to be. But the uncle was superstitious and afraid of the envious. He would not admit strangers to the factory, paid his workforce well and forbade them to let slip even a single word about the secret of making ice.

He had a small department that also manufactured sweet, aromatic and very colourful ice cream – though only in the summer. The round cold lollies were called 'Eskimo', and because it rhymed, you soon heard the Italian word 'primo' along with it in a ditty. When the children heard 'Eskimo primo' in the summer they ran after the vendor in his attractive blue uniform. Hala's father insisted on his vendors being extremely well turned out. They all wore the same uniform and carried a huge thermos filled with the delicious ice cream. Once these containers had soon proved to be insufficient, the vendors could be seen walking behind handsome carts which were equipped with two or three ice cream containers and had silver domes that resembled churches and mosques. Everywhere the vendor appeared, people crowded around him.

Yet Hala's father had intended the ice cream more as an advertisement than a source of income. He had several horse-drawn insulated wagons that his employees used to deliver blocks of ice to his customers. Restaurants, cafés, butchers, greengrocers and ice cream shops all purchased in large quantities for their own use and were, at the same time, sales outlets where the neighbourhood could obtain small chunks of ice. When a family was having people round, the children scurried out with a towel to get a piece of ice from the shop, which the hostess then smashed into splinters to chill the drinks for her guests. The blocks of ice were inexpensive. You shoved the larger pieces into a well-insulated wooden cupboard, thus transforming it into a refrigerator, which would extend the life of your groceries. Butchers were also grateful for this means of preventing their produce rapidly going off.

Everything went well until the beginning of the 1960s, when Hala married a competent employee of her father's and together they soon took over running the business. Her father died confident that he had secured his daughter's future with that factory. But time made what was still a completely new invention seem suddenly outdated. Neither Hala's energy nor her husband's competence could halt the march of progress, which was running against the ice factory.

When every house received its own electricity supply, the fate of the business was sealed. At first they reduced the factory's size, but by the end of the 1960s, Hala and her husband had to close it down. They emigrated to Canada in May of 1970. One month after their arrival, Hala and her husband drowned during an outing on a river.

We were good friends, Hala and I. She was ten years older, but we got along like two sisters. She was clever. She had an odd appearance. Now, from a distance, I can describe her better. She was like a gentle bear. A rounded and shy woman with the strength of a she-bear, she looked so gentle that you had to ask yourself why you should not give such a cuddly animal a hug. That was Hala. She could push three men against the wall and eat for another four, but when she sat there, laughing quietly and talking shyly, one would have thought she was helpless.

When Hala came to visit us, she would want to eat either my stuffed vine leaves or mother's mujadarra. Our mother really liked Hala, because she always arranged for her to have a large block of ice delivered for free. Mother would take half of it for her kitchen and distribute the other half amongst the neighbours.

But when I went to see Hala, I always asked her to make a bean dish. Here is one of the tastiest variations.

فاصوليــاء مع البــاذنجان *

Green beans with garlic and aubergine

*This is one of the delicacies of Damascus. Nowhere else is it as
popular as in my city.*

*Damascenes use a special variety of beans for this, called Lubia
in Arabic. They are also sold as Kenya green beans and are
marked by the intense flavour of the pod and their tiny kernels.
You can also use young French green beans.*

*In this very carefully composed dish, garlic is used as a vegetable
rather than a spice.*

1 large onion
100 ml olive oil
1 large head of garlic
1 kg fresh green beans
Salt and pepper
1 tsp oregano
500 g small, young aubergines (eggplant)
200 ml sunflower oil

*Peel the onion, dice into small cubes and fry for 5 minutes in the
heated olive oil over medium heat. Peel the garlic cloves (at least
15), add whole to the onion and fry another minute. Wash the
beans, snap off the stems and add to the onion mixture, frying a
further 2 minutes. Add salt, pepper and oregano, 100 ml water
and cover to cook for 10 minutes over lowest heat. Then set the
beans aside covered.*

*Trim the aubergine stems to about 1 cm. Trim the leaves back
a bit but do not cut them off entirely as they help hold the
aubergine together. Starting from the stem, peel the aubergine*

in strips and put in salt water for about 5 minutes. Heat the
sunflower oil in a pan. Remove the aubergines from the salt
water and blot dry with a kitchen towel, then fry until crispy
brown in the oil. If the aubergines are too large, slice them after
peeling, in which case you should remove both ends completely.

Blot the fried aubergines on kitchen towel.

❊ *Combine the beans, garlic cloves and aubergines and season*
to taste.

White bread goes well with this.

The salt protects the aubergines from turning brown, draws
out the bitterness and prevents their soaking up too much oil
during frying.

The 'Anbar House', one of the pearls of Damascene residential architecture, is not far from Hala's house. Many of these lovely houses have been converted and are now damaged. A few of them – thank God – have been lovingly restored. The largest house, which we will come to at the end of our stroll, is the Azem Palace near the Umayyad Mosque. But the houses of Naasan, Maktab Anbar, Habib, Yazgi, Shami, Shem'ayya, Leshbona, Quwatli, Barudi, Islambuli, Nizam and as-Sibai are also jewels. The first seven are in the Christian-Jewish Quarter, the last five in the Muslim quarter. Most of these houses have an unbelievably turbulent and moving history. They have seen the rise and fall of dynasties. All the rulers of the world have been guests in them. Conspiracies have been hatched here, which have often become part of world history.

In Naasan House, at the Eastern Gate, you will find the names of American presidents next to those of kings of Asia and Africa. As I have already mentioned, Kaiser Wilhelm II lived in Shami House near the Bab Touma Quarter during his stay in Damascus. The first European embassy in the history of Syria was in Quwatli House: the diplomatic mission of Great Britain.

Anbar House, which we are standing in front of, has a tragic history.

A rich Jew named Jusef Anbar wanted to build himself a majestic masterpiece. He was a handsome rake. Stories of his lust for life circulated amongst the Damascenes. He was not a religious man and quite often travelled to Europe.

So he combined all the styles of the world in his house. Rococo consorted with Baroque and both with Ottoman-Damascene architecture. In 1867 the rich merchant had just started construction, when suddenly the Sultan in Istanbul seized his assets and the Ottoman state carried on with the building. No one really knows what happened, or why, or how. One rumour had it that Jusef Anbar had forgotten for just a moment how minorities are eyed with envy. He is supposed to have said the ruinous sentence, 'I am not building a house, but rather a paradise that has no equal.' This came to the ears of the Ottoman administrator in Damascus, who hated the Jews and the Christians. He and a few other jealous types egged on the Sultan in Istanbul, who needed little reason or justification for expropriating the property of a member of a minority.

Anbar was ruined. The official claim that Anbar was dispossessed because he owed the Sultan money is a lie, as the Sultan never gave money to anyone from the minorities. He always took their money instead. It's difficult to deny the theory that the Jewish merchant's unimaginably huge confiscated fortune was used to finance the expensive build. How else could an almost bankrupt state have paid for nineteen years' work building a private home, adorning the palace with unbelievably expensive decoration and finishing it to the last detail, when the government could not afford to pay for water pipes and a sewage system?

The masterpiece was finally completed in 1886, almost 19 years after construction started, following the plans of the original designer. It was no longer called *Dar* (house) *Anbar*, but *Maktab* (school) *Anbar* and opened as a school for young men in 1886. The first plots by Arab nationalists against the Turks were to be hatched there, and even later, this incredible house would become a school for girls. Today, well restored, it is the home of the Department of Antiquities. Cultural events take place there every now and again.

Step out of Anbar House and go left, and you will end up back on Straight Street, where shops of all kinds are packed in one after the other all the way to the Spice Market Street, al-Bzouriyya, and the streets throb with activity. But, to be honest, unless I am looking to buy something specific, I don't find the area very interesting. Today I am going for a walk with you, and there is better on offer elsewhere.

A few steps farther along you can turn into an alley. Carry on along this alley as it curves to the right and after about 50 metres you reach Aunt Hanan's house. She is a distant cousin of our mother's and I always enjoy visiting her because she is funny and a great hostess. Hers is the only house where I have the strange feeling that I am the owner of the house and she the guest. She opens all her doors and cupboards to you, just as she opens her heart.

Aunt Hanan has three daughters: Siham, Lamis and Balqis, all three of whom live with her in her large Arabic house in the middle of the Muslim part of the Old City. The house has two upper storeys, and surrounds a pretty courtyard. Aunt Hanan and Lamis, her favourite daughter, live on the ground floor. The other two daughters, Siham and Balqis, live on the first floor with their husbands and children. The second floor is small and remains empty. Aunt Hanan does not want any tenants and so she uses the lovely flat at the top as a box room.

The house has been beautifully preserved and, as the rich of Damascus are becoming ever more sophisticated, Aunt Hanan could get millions for it. The daughters would have liked to sell the house and used their share to finance a new-build flat. But Aunt Hanan has repeatedly said: 'When you have carried my dead body out the front door and to the cemetery – then you can sell the house.'

The house lies in the middle of the Muslim Quarter. The residential areas of Damascus used to be divided by religion. Only exceptionally would a Jew or Christian live amongst the Muslims or vice versa. Since the beginning of the 1950s, however, the capital city has undergone a change. The borders have blurred and tangled. Migration into the cities has swollen the population of Damascus ten fold in the last fifty years.

During times of drought farmers have sought their salvation here in massive numbers, making Damascus ever more rustic as a result. You can see it very clearly in photographs. A short time ago I compared some pictures from the 1960s with more recent photos. I have to say: Damascus then was a medium-sized city with a population of about 300,000; today it is an enormous village of over three million farmers. Everything – morals, how people deal with each other, way of life – has become more rural, even as the city's inhabitants try to disguise themselves with fancy cars, satellite dishes and mobile phones.

The gentle mistress or
Of delicate handwriting and strong women

My mother spoke all the time of Aunt Hanan's kindness. As a child I always thought they were sisters because they got on so well. But Hanan is only a cousin many times removed. In her you can see the wisdom in the Arabic saying: Many a brother was not born to your mother. The reverse is usually the case: Your mother rarely bears you a true sister or a true brother.

Hanan's husband, Gibran, was one of the first tram drivers in Damascus. When you go through Damascus today, you will not find a trace of the trams anymore; yet it was once impossible to imagine the streetscape without them. They are a big loss as far as I am concerned. They were attractive, practical, safe, did not stink and provided a service to the community. Gibran died of cancer about ten years ago.

Aunt Hanan inherited from her family many years ago, and has been a clever businesswoman ever since she has been able to think for herself. She owns a lovely house and has earned good money from spices for several decades. Her husband admired her, but did not have a clue when it came to finances. He even put his salary in her hands at the end of the month. He was amazed his entire life that Hanan, though from a wealthy family, had chosen him.

The spice story is a crazy one. For months Hanan went to the market every day, buying small amounts of spices from different dealers, taking advice, assessing the people who worked there and then returning home.

She said there is nothing worse than trying to make a choice amongst people who are all fast talkers.

She searched for half a year before she met a young employee of a large spice shop. His name was Salman. 'He knew everything there is to know about spices and he had a terrific nose,' she explained. 'But he didn't have a single lira in his pocket.'

She had the money.

Her offer to him was: her money, his nose and knowledge. Salman gave her his hand and this handshake was their contract for over 50 years. Salman was not only diligent and loyal. He also always tried to show Aunt Hanan his gratitude. His shop soon became one of the city's essential shopping destinations.

Now he is a venerable old gentleman. He retired a long time ago but you still see him at the market every day. He will join us later and tell us all about the spices. I have already told him about our walk and he is delighted to spend a whole day telling me about spices, whose secrets I will then send to you.

Despite being able to tell fascinating stories, and being clever and capable in life, Aunt Hanan is a lousy cook. No, the kitchen was never her arena. She admired my mother for her culinary abilities, but they remained alien to her. Her three daughters are all the more amazing, unless you agree with Khalil Gibran, the famous Lebanese poet and philosopher, who wrote, more or less, that he learned modesty from an arrogant man, generosity from a miser, humility from a haughty man, gentleness from angry man, and so on, and the wondrous thing is that he is not grateful to his teachers. Aunt Hanan's daughters may have come by their cooking talents by a similar means.

Let us begin with Lamis, who lives with her husband and mother on the ground floor. Lamis is childless, but she lives happily with her husband, who is a bookkeeper in a state-owned tobacco factory. He is a funny man, albeit sometimes too sarcastic and bitter. He respects his wife but idolises and adores his mother-in-law. Hanan had always wanted a son and then all of a sudden Lamis brought her one, without Hanan having to change his nappies. The other two sons-in-law mock him as the 'biggest baby in the world', but they are probably a little jealous, not least because they are worried about being at a disadvantage in matters of inheritance. Lamis herself is something of a stoic, almost uninterested: she seems to sag more than her sisters and has a look of disappointment in her eye.

If Lamis were ever to open a restaurant, its fame would be based primarily on aubergines and it would have to be called 'The Aubergine'. Lamis makes the best Makdus, specially spiced pickled aubergines. These tiny aubergines, which grow in the vegetable gardens of Damascus and are no larger than 8–10 cm, are stuffed with walnuts, paprika and garlic, and preserved in olive oil. They are a Damascene delicacy. Their preparation is complicated, which is why all commercially made Makdus taste awful, whereas Lamis's pickled aubergines flatter the palate.

She is the master not only of such fancy dishes: her aubergines are unusually tasty even in quite ordinary dishes. I used to think aubergines were boring until Lamis showed me what she does with them. Since then I find the exotic looking fruit simply exquisite.

Puréed aubergine is a particularly popular starter, which is as filling as any heavy meat dish. Lamis makes the purée in three different variations, which are all related to each other but offer different flavours.

Many Damascenes fry aubergines in order to use them for the purée. Lamis fundamentally rejects that. The flavour of the aubergine in a purée only begins to assert itself when it has been baked beforehand. Of course you can fry aubergines on occasion. They taste terrific. But the flavour of the frying oil kills all the nuances of the vegetable in the purée.

✳ متبل الباذنجان ✳
Aubergine Purée

1 kg aubergines
4 garlic cloves
Salt and pepper
½ lemon

1 small bunch of parsley
50 ml olive oil

The aubergines must be firm and smooth, and the stem as well as the blossom seat must be green, fresh and appear crisp.
Do not peel the aubergines. Wash them and pierce them several times with a fork so the steam can escape from inside the aubergine – otherwise the fruit might explode in the oven. Bake the aubergines on a charcoal grill or in an oven, turning them frequently. The skin will turn coal black, which is why this dish is also called 'Priest' in some places. Bake until the flesh is soft, which takes about ½ hour. Plunge in cold water. Cut off the stem end and pull the skin back from the cut toward the other end of the aubergine. If the peel pulls flesh away with it, place the strips of skin on a cutting board and carefully scrape away the flesh with the back of a knife and put in the bowl. The meat just under the charred skin tastes smoky and gives the dish its wonderful, unique aroma. Mash the peeled aubergines in a bowl or purée in a food processor. Peel the garlic and mash with some salt or crush and add salt, pepper and lemon juice.

Remove the stems from the parsley, wash and chop.

Place the purée on a large plate and spread to a smooth layer about 2 cm thick using a spoon or broad knife. Sprinkle the chopped parsley on top and drizzle with a thin stream of olive oil. If you wish, you can also sprinkle a few pome-granate seeds over the top.

Serve with bread.

❊ *In Damascus, all variations of puréed aubergine are called Mutabbal, Arabic for spiced, to suggest the complexity of spices some might add to it. Lamis is very wary of this, however, as, in her opinion, too much spice can mean the unique taste of the aubergine is lost.*

Aubergine Purée with Yoghurt
Before you add the parsley and olive oil, mix 100 g of yoghurt into the purée to create a refreshing variation.

Aubergine Purée with Sesame Paste
Prepare as above but instead of using half a lemon, use a whole one and mix its juice with 4 tbsp of sesame paste (the off-white viscous liquid called tahini, not the clear sesame oil!). Add 1 tbsp of water and mix it all together thoroughly. A milky liquid will develop which is stirred into the aubergine purée, along with the garlic, salt and pepper. Only then do you add the parsley and olive oil.

I have no contact with the second daughter, Balqis. We do not like each other – I do not like her and she does not like me. So be it.

The third daughter, Siham, is kindness personified. She has suffered quite a bit because she was active in a leftist underground party. She was arrested and went to jail for five years. But her husband kept faith with her and admired her courage. He is a teacher and is totally peaceable in his disposition. His name is *Nimr*, Tiger, but he is more like a camel, placid yet robust. She is not. For all her goodness, she is the born impatient fighter. And that is also how she is raising her three children. This often leads to tension between her and Nimr, who has been trying to teach them to love peace and your enemy in the true Christian manner. They are a remarkable couple I always enjoy visiting. You never feel bored there and never have to feign interest.

Siham is not allowed to work as a teacher anymore, so she now works at home as a translator of French novels. She also gives private French lessons on the side. Fewer students are calling on her, as French is out of fashion, and the publishers pay a miserable amount, but she enjoys the work.

Siham's husband is a great expert in matters of calligraphy, the art of visualising a language with lines. Nimr can sit quietly for hours writing beautiful sayings in cursive script. Watching him, you notice how calm his hand and soul are. Arabic writing must be laid out according to complicated stylistic rules. Word and script are powerful things for Arabs. The desert is responsible for this.

The desert, the ancient home of mankind, shaped its people, having both a positive and negative impact on their culture. The Arabs' love for language is unique to them and the weight of the word in Arab culture is unsurpassed by any other culture.

In European Christianity, the word of God became flesh in Jesus. In Islam, the word of God became a book, the Koran. Here is the most impressive demonstration of the endless respect Arabs have for the word. The first word in the Koran is not 'see' or 'God', but 'read'. As a matter of fact, the word Koran (Arabic *Qur'an*) means reading.

The significance of language in Arabian culture contrasts with the weakness of Arabic painting. People like to hide behind Islam's law forbidding the production of likenesses, but that is not the decisive factor. As we have already discussed, Arab culture had not given rise to any great skill in painting and sculpture even before the advent of Islam.

Despite this reverence for the word, there was no occupation Muhammad condemned more than that of the poet – but what effect did that have? Arabs since the time of Mohammad have written some of the most beautiful poetry in the world.

The desert gave the Arabs little opportunity to train their eyes for painting, but it gave them all the more time for the fabulous development of their tongues. The Arabs, practically dying of thirst and half starved, used the beauty and power of the word to paint a paradise on earth. They drew in colour with words and found nuance upon nuance of which no painter's brush is capable. The barrenness of their environment produced wealth in the imagination and in the words in which it found expression.

As the word is so powerful in Arab culture, they have cultivated the art of arranging words on the page. The Japanese are the only other culture on earth to have developed a similar philosophy of the art of writing. All mosques, books and palaces were decorated with calligraphy. But – an entire book could be written about calligraphy. What am I saying? Nimr has an entire wall of bookshelves filled with lovely old and new volumes about Arab calligraphy. It was Nimr who gave me the most beautiful explanation of the different styles of writing. For him, there is no 'back' and 'front' in a script. 'Arabs, Aramaeans, Persians and Jews,' he told me with a smile, 'write from right to left, from the right hand toward the heart.'

I thought this was curious. 'And the Europeans?' I asked jokingly.

'They write from left to right, from the heart outward toward mankind.'

'And the Japanese and Chinese?'

'They write from the heavenly to the earthly.'

Siham enjoys cooking and entertaining. Her love of courgettes simply amazes me. This vegetable is not much respected in Damascus. Apparently courgettes have suffered from their similarity to cucumbers, their milder, almost neutral flavour and their plentiful harvest. Courgettes are dead cheap. But Siham likes to use them nevertheless as a base for a number of delicious dishes. These are all (except one of them) easy to cook and very healthy.

❋ حساء الكوسا البارد المنعش ❋
Cold Courgette Soup
A really tasty starter that you can make in just 10 minutes...

500 g fresh courgettes (the smaller the better)
250 g plain yoghurt, cream or crème fraîche
Chopped mint and basil leaves (as much or as little as you like)
2 tsp salt
1 tsp ground black pepper
50 g pine kernels

Rinse the courgettes in cold water and trim at both ends. Dice into large cubes and mix in a large, deep bowl along with the washed and finely chopped basil and mint. Stir in the yoghurt (or cream), add salt and ground pepper and using a hand blender puree to a smooth, creamy consistency. If the mixture is too thick, just add more yoghurt or cream, and finish with a squeeze of lemon juice. Lightly toast the pine kernels.

If it's a hot day, let the soup stand in the fridge for 1 hour. To serve, spoon into soup bowls or wide, flat dishes. Garnish with a sprinkling of basil leaves or pine kernels (or both) – the soup will be thick enough for them to rest on top without sinking.

Served with chunks of crispy French bread, this soup makes a substantial light lunch all on its own.

❋ كوسى مع الجوز ❋

Courgettes with walnuts

1 bunch parsley
100 ml olive oil
1 large onion
1 kg courgettes (zucchini)
2 garlic cloves
1 tsp allspice
½ tsp salt
100 g walnuts

Remove stems and yellow leaves from the parsley, wash and finely chop.

Heat oil in a frying pan. Peel the onions, chop finely and add to the pan. Fry for 5 minutes. Cut both ends off the courgettes, wash and finely slice. Add to the onions and fry for another 5 minutes over medium heat. Peel and crush the garlic into the courgettes. Add the spices and walnuts and fry for a further

2 minutes over low heat. Turn off the heat, add the chopped
parsley to the courgettes and serve with white bread.

✳ كوسى محشي ✳
Stuffed Courgettes

This is the king of all courgette dishes. To achieve an attractive
result demands practice, but the flavour is exquisite, so it is
definitely worth giving it a try. The courgettes must be hollowed
out, leaving a 2–3 mm thick wall. Best for this is a special knife
(Minkar in Arabic) that has a blade in the shape of a long thin
half cylinder. You can also use an apple corer or a small spoon.
By the way, the stuffing is also delicious in hollowed out sweet
peppers, potatoes, pumpkins or aubergines.

The Meat Filling
100 g butterfat
50 g pine nuts
2 large onions
500 g beef mince
2 garlic cloves
1 tsp allspice
½ tsp cinnamon
½ tsp paprika
Salt and pepper

Heat the butterfat in a frying pan, and fry the pine nuts to a
light brown. Remove. Peel the onions and finely dice. Fry them
to golden yellow in the fat. Add the meat and fry another 5
minutes. Peel the garlic and mash with salt or crush directly
onto the meat in the pan. Stir once, add all the spices and fry
for another 2 minutes over low heat.

Turn off the heat and stir in the fried pine nuts. Allow the
filling to cool.

The Sauce

3 tbsp tomato paste
200 ml water
1 tsp salt
1 tsp dried mint
2 garlic cloves
1 tbsp butterfat

Stir the tomato paste into the water. Add salt and mint and
stir. Peel the garlic cloves and briefly fry in preheated butter fat
(do not let them darken). Immediately pour tomato sauce on it.
It is best for this dish to use 1 kg of small, young courgettes – no
larger than 10 to 12 cm – with a light, firm skin. Most Arabic
or Turkish grocers carry them.

Cut off the stem and then carefully hollow out the fruit bit
by bit to leave a tube no thicker than 2 to 3 mm. Wash the
courgettes and stuff them with the meat filling. Place the
courgettes closely packed in a saucepan so that the open end
is pressed against the side of the pan or another courgette
to prevent the filling from coming out. Pour the sauce over
them and leave to simmer over a low heat for 15 minutes. The
courgettes should still have a bit of bite to them.

❄ Should the hollowing out prove too difficult, simply halve
the courgettes lengthwise, scrape out the flesh and replace with
the stuffing. Or, finely dice the courgettes, fry, mix with the
meat, pour the sauce over and allow to simmer for only 10
minutes over the lowest heat.

Rice, as well as spaghetti or tagliatelli, go well with this.

❄ Some like the stuffing even better with rice added to it.
(This does not work well, however, if you are using the filling in
potatoes.)

Coming out of Aunt Hanan's house and turning right soon brings us to the well-restored Nizam House, which I mentioned earlier in my list of the most beautiful houses in Damascus. There is another fine example of Damascene residential architecture nearby: as-Sibai House. If you continue from there you run into Hassan Kharet Street, which begins at the southern gate of the Old City, Bab al Saghir, and ends at Straight Street. Its continuation on the other side of the junction is called Souq al Bzouriyya, the Spice Market, which leads to the greatest concentration of beautiful and historic buildings anywhere in Damascus.

If you turn right at the junction of Straight Street and Hassan Kharet, you will be heading east, back towards the Bab Sharqi Quarter, in which we have already spent quite a bit of time. If you turn left, toward the west, then you will be walking under a vaulted roof from here along the rest of Straight Street all the way to its endpoint at the Bab al Jabiye Gate. The covered part of the street contains many shops and sights that are described in great detail in any tourist guide, but are not of interest for our stroll.

Such roofs, which can be found in many of Damascus's streets, alleys and markets, serve primarily to protect visitors from the great heat (or sometimes rain), so that they can pursue unimpeded their favourite occupation – haggling. This particular roof was once made of wood, but after numerous devastating fires it was rebuilt with load-bearing beams made of iron and a roof of weather-resistant zinc plate.

After a great Syrian uprising against the French occupation in 1925, the French air force fired on the civilian population with machine guns. You can still see the bullet holes in the roof today. Strangely enough, they give the roof the appearance of a star-filled sky.

But now we have to hurry, as Salman is waiting to tell us all about the secrets of spices.

Al Bzouriyya, or
Of playing notes on the palate

The word *souq*, or *suq*, means commercial street or area. Originally, though, the word meant to lead. So, the market is that place to which wares (including camels and sheep) are led in order to be sold. The word *bazaar* is Persian and means the same thing. As a rule, a souq consists of a number of large and small alleys. Like a mosque, it belongs to the image of an Arabian city. It is not always clear why the souqs in a city are arranged the way they are. Damascus has preserved a classical distribution: starting from the mosque and moving out toward the fringe districts of the city the merchandise becomes ever coarser. Near the mosque you will find books, paper, precious metals, spices, perfume and expensive fabrics. Situated the farthest away are the smelly and noisy shops which sell animal fodder, animals, leather and copper containers.

Damascus has been lucky. It is one of the few Arabic or Middle Eastern cities where the souq has not become a tourist trap, as in Istanbul or Marrakech. The souq here continues to survive on the sale of essential merchandise to people from the city and surrounding areas. It is as colourful as ever, but not at all prettified, and its air is thick with the most incredible variety of smells.

The arrangement of souqs according to the wares that are sold there has deep historical roots but it is practically incomprehensible to a European. When looking at 50 shops, densely packed side-by-side in the same alley and selling all the same goods, a European will wonder how their owners can compete and survive.

All shops dealing in a particular category of merchandise were collected in one street, alley or area in order to be able to provide them with better protection and to control them better. There were markets for silk, wool, wood, copper, spices, gold and leather. There were also special markets for every trade: one for locksmiths, one for tailors, one for glaziers and many more. Of course each area of Damascus was up to a point self-sufficient, having its own bakery, its own grocers and other important kinds of shop, but it was in the large souqs that the best selection of suppliers could be found.

The Spice Market is one of the most interesting markets the city of Damascus has to offer. In Arabic, the street is called *Bzouriyya* (kernel and seed market). The Spice Market also has a metal roof that enables passers-by, buyers and sellers to look and trade undisturbed. Heavy demands are made on your eyes, nose and ears.

The scent of a peculiar mixture of perfume, sweat and spices fills the nose. The eye cannot rest for all the constant movement, colour and the many cones of light shining down picturesquely on the goods from little holes in the roof. Shouts and all manner of noises tumble over each other and compete to be heard by the passers-by.

Experienced Damascenes can spot their friends and acquaintances with amazing ease amongst the crowds of people and salute them with a brief greeting or smile. They are able to pick up the smallest hint of a specific spice in amongst the numbing jumble of smells and follow it to where it is being sold. From among the multi-coloured, eye-dazzling array of offers they can find their desired sweet, longed-for material, or appropriate nuts or blends of spices, stopping to look, taste or test with an enviable calm while the maelstrom continues around them.

Salman, who was Aunt Hanan's business partner and our spice merchant for many years, is a walking encyclopaedia in all matters spice, as we have mentioned before. You only have to mention a name and he will begin to tell you everything you need to know about that spice. Sometimes he stands, now a sprightly old man, in front of a heap of pepper, coriander or cardamom as he used to. He takes a pinch with his trembling hand and looks at it lovingly, as if he were telling it of his yearning. He was the one who explained the origin of the Arabic word *Bihar* or *Behar* to me, and how it was first used for pepper, then for allspice, later for pepper mixtures and then even for spices generally. Bihar is a state in India (in the lower Ganges region). The spices were given the name of a state that was known for its aromatic seeds and roots.

There have long been debates about when humans first began using spices to please their palates and to preserve food. Some count the use of spices amongst the first signs of the development of a civilised society. Salman goes so far as to claim that the ancient religions burned incense in their temples in order to transmit a touch of godliness by way of the nose, a practice later adopted by the Catholic Church.

Knowledge of spices is ancient. The Egyptians used many herbs, spices and oils. By 1600 BC they were at least as familiar with anise, cardamom, mustard, sesame and cumin, as they were with frankincense and myrrh. Camel trains laden with spices travelled from Ethiopia and the Arabian Peninsula along the Red Sea to Damascus, from where the spices carried on northwards over land and sea to Europe.

Its vital position on these caravan routes made Damascus wealthy. With that in mind, the dealers kept the sources and whereabouts of their goldmine, 'Spice', secret, and often invented tales of the horrible creatures that made obtaining the spices so difficult and thus drove their prices up. They did this even if the herbs and spices were indigenous to the Middle East, like coriander, thyme, sumac, sesame and other fragrant plants. For a time, the lies paid off: pepper was more valuable than gold.

Salman talked to me for eight hours about spices. I have summarised his remarks and put them in alphabetical order for ease of reference.

Allspice
One of the newest arrivals in the Arabian kitchen, allspice comes from the New World (Jamaica) and now enjoys broad popularity because it seems to combine several spices both in its aroma and it flavour. Its mild sharpness is reminiscent of pepper, its smell a mixture of nutmeg, cloves

and cinnamon. It is also inexpensive. It is often used in meat dishes, such as the ever popular meat pie, Kibbeh. It is also included in many other spice mixtures on offer in Damascus.

Anise

The streets of the Old City of Damascus not only have their own distinctive architecture, they also each have their own smells, determined by the warehouses, trades or distilleries that have developed all over the city. Our Abbara Alley smells of anise because there is a large warehouse there in which anise is cleaned and packed in jute sacks for export to Europe.

The yellow-green to grey-green aniseeds are traded as a spice but they are rarely used as such. Anise is popular in some biscuits and bonbons but its primary role is as the main ingredient in the popular Damascene anise schnapps, Arak. It is the anise in Arak that gives the drink its lovely milky appearance when water is added.

Cardamom

Some spices have an unrivalled prestige, and cardamom is one of them. It is the prince amongst spices and in some places it is also called the 'seeds of paradise'. It is claimed to have miraculous effects on digestion.

The brownish black cardamom seeds are of the best quality when the pods are green and dry. Light-coloured pods are either old and less aromatic or have been bleached with sulphur dioxide to give the false impression that they have been sun ripened and so will last longer, which is all grotesque nonsense. Green cardamom capsules have the best fragrance and keep a long time anyway when stored dry. Many shops also offer cardamom powder, but as a rule this is bogus and contains more peels and substitutes than real cardamom seeds.

Cardamom is used in coffee either as whole pods or ground. Experts claim that Cardamom reduces the damaging effects of caffeine. You can chew the seeds for a good flavour and to freshen your mouth, but this requires some getting used to, as cardamom tastes strangely pungent and almost numbingly cool at first bite. However it soon unfolds its typical, ethereally warming taste. Cardamom supposedly sharpens memory.

Aside from coffee, and in contrast to Indian cooking, cardamom is used in Arabia only in a few meat or chicken dishes, and, unlike in Europe, it is unusual to use it in cakes or baked goods.

Cinnamon

The ancient Egyptians were already familiar with the disinfectant qualities of cinnamon – they used it for embalming their dead. Yet it was also treasured as a perfume in ancient times. It is difficult to imagine today that in those days, as reported by the Bible, beds were perfumed with the sweet woody scent of cinnamon (Proverbs 7:17). At that time the bark of the exotic cinnamon tree, which originally came from the tropical forests of Sri Lanka and grew up to 10 metres in height, was already highly valued. The spice is made from the bark of twigs, which is hand-rolled at great cost into small rods that are then unrolled and rerolled daily until they dry out.

Cinnamon has a variety of uses in Arabian cooking. In addition to sweets, cinnamon is also used regularly in preparing chicken and lamb. It is also a classic ingredient in curry powder.

Coriander

Coriander grows practically like a weed in the Middle East. It is a modest annual plant that thrives in virtually every climate. Coriander came to prominence in ancient Egypt and, through a translation error, was compared to manna from heaven (Exodus 16:31). The seeds have absolutely nothing in common with snow white, sweet manna but apparently the Greek translators were not that particular.

The fresh leaves and, still more frequently, the seeds are used to flavour dishes. Dried leaves are also available, but they tend to taste strange. The ground seeds smell sweet, but also faintly of pepper and taste pleasantly mild. Coriander is found in every second Damascene spice mixture and is used to season spinach, mince, lamb and lentil dishes.

Cumin

Cumin has been known about for a very long time. It has had similar-sounding names as far back as Akkadian (*kemum*), Arabic (*kamum*) and Hebrew (*kamon*).

In powdered form Damascenes use it as a spice in bean dishes, chickpea purée and meat dishes. Cumin smells fabulous. It is said that it is the ruler amongst fragrances, not because it smells better, but because it smells so strongly. Its oil is often used in perfumes. Cumin gives Middle Eastern markets their typical aroma. Yet some people do not care for it, declaring that it smells a bit too mouldy to them. That perception is not entirely amiss, as Cumin has a sour top note that overlays its actual sweet fragrance. Its flavour is unique and distinctive. Cumin is hot, but without a lasting effect on the tongue.

Garlic

There can scarcely be another plant that, since ancient times, has caused such long-lasting and irreconcilable argument. You are either friend or foe. In Boccaccio, a lover woos his beloved with a bulb of garlic and is successful but many a relationship has broken up because one member of it could no longer tolerate this third partner, who would climb into bed with the couple, stay the night and make himself unpleasantly noticeable again first thing in the morning.

Garlic belongs to the lily family and is related to onions, shallots, leeks and chives. The bulb has been known for millennia. The ancient Indians, Sumerians, Egyptians and Greeks used it. Herodotus reported that the workers who built the pyramid of Cheops always went on strike when they did not receive their garlic ration. The Greeks ascribed to it an ability to increase physical strength and so gave it to their soldiers. The Romans even claimed it had aphrodisiac qualities. Such claims aside, there is no question that garlic disinfects and has a cleansing effect on blood. It is also supposed to lower blood pressure.

Garlic grows in many countries, but it first reached Europe by way of Arabia.

It is widely used in Syrian cooking, but not to the point of intoxication, as in other eastern cuisines. The Damascene tongue prefers intimation to harsh clarity. Eating green herbs such as parsley, thyme or marjoram afterwards can supposedly reduce the odour of garlic.

Mint

These days mint is called *na'na'* in Damascus, a word of Persian origin perhaps. It used to be called *nammam*, which means something like telltale, because mint gives away its location through its scent. The plant will grow in the wild, provided only that it gets enough water. It has many different varieties.

It is easy to understand why mint, with its pleasant scent and its sweet-bitter, mild flavour, was discovered early on in the Mediterranean area. Egyptians and Greeks added it to beer for fragrance and used extracts from it in beauty care. According to Greek mythology the nymph Menthe was transformed into mint. And we learn from the New Testament (Luke 11:42 and Matthew 23:23) that taxes were levied on mint.

In Damascus, mint is often added fresh in generous quantities to salads. Its dried form also has many uses in the kitchen.

There is a good reason why mint is popular in the city: its ethereal aroma, which derives mostly from menthol, has a cooling and refreshing effect and so is wonderfully suited for the hottest days in Damascus. Even meat dishes that are quite hearty gain a certain lightness with the addition of small quantities of mint.

Mint is also drunk as tea and is very popular added to black tea. You take a fresh leaf, place it in the glass and fill up with tea.

Nigella

The Damascenes call this 'blessing seed'. They sprinkle it on the special bread that is only baked during the holy month of Ramadan and is very similar to Turkish bread (pitta), hoping that this will bless the bread. That is how the loveliest name this spice ever had came about and that is why it should be called that in all languages. No other spice has been so chaotically and confusingly named as this darling of the Arabic kitchen. The teacher, whoever he was, who allowed names such strange and misleading names as 'black sesame', 'black caraway', or 'black anise' must have been useless. Even the translators of the Bible made an error here, translating the Hebrew *ketzah* (Arabic *kazha*) as dill instead of nigella. Botanically speaking, the plant is as closely related to these as a blade of grass is to a palm tree. It belongs to the Nigella family, whose plants have pretty, delicate flowers and names like 'Love-in-a-Mist'. The seeds of other plants in the Nigella family are often inedible.

In Damascus the spice is used for specific breads and also for sheep's cheese. Nigella intensifies the flavour of sheep's cheese, so the Damascenes sprinkle it on the cheese and then drizzle olive oil on top, to give the salty cheese a noble taste.

Nigella tastes tart and smells weakly aromatic. When you bite down on the seeds, though, it releases a breath reminiscent of lavender, mint, marjoram and pepper.

Nutmeg

Nowadays nutmeg is widely used in Damascene cooking. It smells and tastes best when grated directly from the nut just before use, so that the nut releases a strong sweet aroma. In Damascus, nutmeg is used primarily in lamb dishes, because it dispels certain unpleasant odours of the meat, particularly if the butcher has erred in the age of the animal.

Oregano

In Arabia, oregano has a different name depending on where you are: mountain mint, wild thyme, wild marjoram, and so on, but all these names have one thing in common: they remind us that this roughly 50 cm high plant grows in the wild. The leaves smell and taste intensely like Marjoram, which is why gourmets prefer oregano to garden-cultivated marjoram. Oregano can also be found in many spice mixtures and is highly recommended for meat or tomato dishes.

Pepper

Pepper's Arabic name, *filfil* or *fulful*, with its repeated first syllable, has a musical sound. There are only a few names in Arabic which repeat the first syllable in the same way: *hudhud* (hoopoe), *sumsum* (sesame), *bulbul* (nightingale). Pepper, along with salt, can be found on every Damascene dining table. Its aroma is not conspicuously strong, but it has a heat known and loved the world over – in Sanskrit, pepper is called *maricha*, one of the names of the sun, which gives an indication of its firepower – and because it is not too overpowering it is suited to many dishes and spice mixtures.

Like many spices, pepper only really reveals its flavour and aroma when it is freshly ground.

Pistachio

The Bible (Genesis 43:11) already mentions pistachios as a treasured gift. Alexander the Great encountered them in Syria. The Romans took them from Syria to Italy and Spain. The ancient Egyptians imported the resin from the trees, which they used in embalming, as well as the seeds.

In addition to pistachios, almonds, pine nuts, peanuts, walnuts and hazelnuts are also well known in the Middle East. But no matter how many nut varieties the Mediterranean has to offer, the pistachio (and if you want to be precise, it is not a nut but rather a seed) remains the queen.

Pistachios are eaten raw as well as roasted. Confectioners and patisseries use the majority in the production of sweets. Cooks from Morocco to Iran may have invented all manner of ways of using the Pistachio, but the Damascenes remain the masters of the secretive art of conjuring up the fantastic pistachio rolls, made from Pistachios, sugar and pasta dough.

Pomegranate

The image of the pomegranate and its crimson blossom is everywhere in Damascus. The Damascenes are familiar with three varieties of pomegranates, those with sweet seeds, those with sweet and sour seeds and those that are sour. The sweet pomegranate is used as a dessert or the juice is squeezed from it and drunk for refreshment. The sweet and sour and the sour pips are used as a garnish on salads and other dishes. Their juice is also often reduced to a thick brown syrup and then used in all manner of dishes. The flavour is acidic and very aromatic. Though Damascenes value this spice highly, vinegar and lemon are beginning to displace the thick pomegranate syrup in Damascene cooking.

The peels used to be collected, dried and used in tanning.

Rosemary

The name sounds as poetic in Arabic as it does in Latin, which lovingly baptised the plant 'Dew of the Sea'. The Arabs called rosemary *iklil aljabal*, the crown of the mountain. When you rub the leaves, it smells like incense.

The leaves are used to flavour meat dishes, and to make tea blends against colds. Rosemary oil, which is extracted from the leaves, is used in the soap industry and is mixed into bath additives and liniments. The ethereal oil from the leaves contains a substance similar to camphor. It is supposed to be invigorating for the circulatory system.

Saffron

There was once a caliph who only loved the colour yellow. He would only wear yellow robes and only allowed yellow flowers to grow in his garden. The wasteful caliph even wanted the artificial little stream winding through the palace garden to be yellow. The watercourse was thus 'rebedded' so that the water actually splashed over saffron-dyed cloths and appeared yellow. Saffron is as valuable as gold. People speak of the saffron blossom, but it is only the stigma or pistil of the saffron crocus that is used. Over 15,000 blossoms have to picked and dried by hand in order to obtain 100 g of real saffron. Safflower is frequently offered at the Spice Market for little money. Safflower is a widely occurring annual with many yellow-orange blossoms. It will colour food yellow like Saffron, but smells and tastes of nothing. That is why those knowledgeable in buying tend to advise against purchasing so-called 'Saffron Powder' as it is usually just made up of the inexpensive safflower. The ancient Egyptians were already planting this substitute 3,000 years ago.

You should purchase saffron as short threads and carefully grind it and mix it in yourself. A tiny amount is sufficient.

Sesame

This annual plant has been known in the Middle East for over 3,000 years. Documents written in cuneiform already reported of it. It was valued particularly where olive trees did not grow well (Babylon). It is easy to plant and fruitful in harvest. The seeds have a neutral odour, but provide a considerable amount of oil that rarely goes rancid and therefore is particularly popular in the heat of the Middle East. The thick opaque purée (*tahini*) is used pure in many dishes, or sometimes with lemon added. Tarator, a popular dip, consists mainly of tahini and lemon. It tastes terrific with fish and meat dishes.

Combining tahini and sugar allowed the Damascenes to invent *halawe*, meaning sweet in Arabic (Turkish Halva). It is the most nutritious of seductions, provided you do not have a weight problem.

Roasted sesame is delicious and is often used in the production of bread, butter biscuits and falafel.

Sumac

The name comes from Aramaic. Sumac is one of the few non-poisonous relatives of the stag's horn sumac. It grows as a bush and is immune to most diseases and insects. Sumac has small compact clusters of tiny reddish berries.

Sumac is a blessed plant. Its leaves have been used in massive quantities in tanneries since ancient times, which led to the wild plant being cultivated in areas suited to it. The Kalamun Mountains of the Anti-Lebanon Range north of Damascus are an ideal area for these plants.

The ripe little berries are harvested in late summer, after which the bush is cut back to the ground. The plant grows back again the following year.

The furry red berries are dried and ground. The powder tastes tart and fruity sour and is widely used in Syria and the Lebanon in all manner of meat, fish and lentil dishes. The Turks use sumac in their world famous dish – doner kebabs.

The most important use of the sumac berry, however, is as a leavening ingredient in Syria's popular spice mixture: zahtar.

Thyme

Over thirty different varieties of thyme are found across Asia, Europe and North Africa. Its strong aroma and its distinctive flavour make it popular in cooking. It is used to season mince, vegetable stews and soups. A touch of thyme intensifies the taste of salad and it is a major component of zahtar – the most famous of Damascene spice mixtures. It is said that thyme is good for bronchial, stomach and intestinal illnesses.

The centuries old superstition that thyme makes children intelligent survives in Damascus. Modern parents laugh about it, spread olive oil on a piece of flat bread and then – just in case, mind you – sprinkle thyme or the beloved zahtar mixture on it for their children. They reject the superstition, but you never know.

Turmeric

This root looks like ginger. Turmeric has an intense aroma, a little like musk, and tastes bitter, with a sharp aftertaste on the tongue. It is frequently used as a substitute for saffron for colouring and seasoning, which is why Turmeric is also called 'poor man's saffron'. Turmeric also plays an important role in curry.

Zahtar

Hardly any other spice mixture is as treasured in Syria as zahtar. It is passed around in little bowls together with small bowls of the best quality olive oil. You dip a piece of bread in the oil and then press it into the mixture. Bread seasoned in this manner stimulates the appetite.

You can also make little flat breads, brush them with a thick paste of olive oil and zahtar, then bake them briefly and serve them as an appetiser or for breakfast.

So what is zahtar? The word actually means thyme, but dried thyme represents at most 20 to 30 per cent of the mixture. The other parts are roasted sesame, roasted and ground pistachio and nuts, paprika, coriander, cumin, allspice and sumac powders, as well as salt. Every city has its own secret recipe. As a result zahtar is sourer in some regions and spicier in others. The high reputation of the blend from Aleppo, *zahtar halabi*, which you can also get in Damascus, is undisputed. If asked, spice traders will mix the components freshly for you, with supreme style.

With so many spices in my head, my soul yearns for something lighter, sweeter. Uncle Faris and his wife, Aunt Malake, are the right people to go to and they live not far from the Spice Market.

...e.

...But

...ided with
...were made
...oring and had
...r parents met up.
...be sad, each of them
...over an endlessly large
...us about each other. Not
...d a single derogatory word
...at business? Not for one sec-
...determination to keep making a
...ered a new aspect of his personality

...o people can be. He was as tall, broad and
..., and she was small and skinny. But as soon
...swapped roles. He was soft and insecure, polite
...s assertive, strong and direct, with no regard for
...r liked her a lot. Father was frequently horrified at
...he never said a word. A good Arab host learns early on
...r tongue.

...s and Malika were capable of drinking quite a lot of schnapps
...never went home before they were drunk. But they never lost
..., not even for a second. They would become wittier, more child-
...and suddenly get the irresistible urge to sing – and they have truly
...astly voices, both of them. Father and Mother laughed a lot with them.
Sometimes I would be lying in bed and hear how all four of them laughed
until they were short of breath.

Everyday miracles or
Of nightingale nests, marzipan and orange blossoms

Life consists of an endless number of miracles that we greet with a gaping jaw on the first occasion, and then get used to. Are we still surprised by our nightly sleep? By dreams? Scientists study black holes in space, yet they do not really know why they sleep, where their dreams come from or where they go to. Many lives are an uninterrupted succession of miracles, great and small.

Our father's good friend, Faris, had an impressive array of miracles at his disposal. Twice he flew to see his only son in London, who had settled there as a chemist and had no desire ever to return to Damascus. Malika, the boy's mother, would not fly, but Faris was so sick with longing for his only son, that he finally flew to visit him ten years ago. In London, the aircraft thundered off the end of the runway and crashed into the fence around the airport. There were 20 dead and over 50 injured. Faris did not have a scratch on him. Not even his suitcase was damaged. He shook off the dust and hurried to the arrivals hall to find his son, who was practically dead with fear.

On the second flight, the wheels could not be lowered and the plane landed on a foam carpet. Once again Faris escaped without injury, while his son was close to a heart attack. He begged his father not to fly to London anymore and has come to Damascus once a year with his English wife ever since. She is a very bright and extremely thoughtful person. I once invited them both around for a meal and during this meal, the son leaned

over and whispered to me, 'Give my regards to your brother in Ger[m]
and gave a short laugh. 'I'd rather not come back here as well. But [
my father smashed up the Brits' last airplane and I ended up griev[i]
sanatorium, I thought it was better that I come over for these fe[w]
each year.' Something about Damascus does not sit right with
contrast, his wife is really keen on the city.

But back to Faris. The bit about the airplanes is sensational
in comparison to the life and love miracle Faris managed to a[

I was a little girl when I first heard of Faris. Father kept
that this man was a very strange restaurant owner. This wa[
new to me. I was familiar with poor and rich, appetising ar
erous and stingy, expert and dilettante, dirty and clean, b
heard of a strange restaurateur. When I questioned him, F[
that Faris was unusual because whenever he has had to s
taurant, he *never* forgets to pay off his debts to his su[
before. That still left a major question mark. Probably
before.

'Faris has already had more than ten,' Father expl[
for Faris and sometimes wanted to give the bankrupt[
delivery for nothing. But Faris would just laugh an[
open another restaurant in a few weeks. This new r[
be the one he had always dreamed of and so it wou[
my father as his baker.

Father was not only a baker of highest reput[
bake flat breads for restaurants, which were a lit[
much as the customers would notice. This help[
to make a small saving when filling them as sandwiches. Witi[
wiches, that small, imperceptible difference can have quite an effect. In
this way, father attracted many restaurants and they were big customers.

Fairly soon Faris would be claiming that the new restaurant he had
longed for was in fact an appalling pit, teeming with snakes in human
form. It appeared that these snakes drank the frying oil, consumed whole
unwashed lettuces in one bite, made tea, petrol, oil, wine, tomato paste

They are a wonderful, witty couple. The initial stiffness and polite
phrases soon gave way to an openhearted conversation. Faris and Malika
are something of a marriage miracle. I know: there's no such thing. There
are 300 tons of poems about unrequited love in Arabia, and not a single
one about a good marriage. That is why this pair count as a miracle to m[
If you were to believe the poems, this couple do not love each other
they certainly enjoy living together.

It was not love at first sight for them. Faris's mother had de[
her best friend – who was Malika's mother – that the tw[
for each other. But the young people found each other [
already as children began to avoid each other when th[
agreed. Then they married and each began to dis[
world in the other, and so they would not [
more, not less. You know, Malika never sa[
about her husband's amateurish attempt[
ond! On the contrary, she admired hi[
new start and insisted that she disc[
with every business collapse.
They were as opposite as t[
strong as a heavyweight box[
as they began talking the[
and deferential. She w[
consequence. Mot[
her openness, but[
how to bite the[
Both Fari[
and they[
contro[
like[

having to clos[
mother. She laughed and rep[
said. Apparently this was what Faris had [
dressed and pressed, with his wife the next day.

When you visited them they were always generous. Their cooking was nothing special. Uncle Faris had lost any inclination for the culinary arts because of the endlessly trashy cooking he had had to do in his restaurants, as he often had to play chef, waiter and cashier at the same time when one of his employees could not be bothered to turn up anymore.

Aunt Malika, his wife, also did not particularly enjoy cooking. That was pretty clear. But you could forgive her this because she had a passion that got every visitor excited: she was an absolute master of sweets. Father once summarised this on the way home: at their house, you eat like a beggar, drink like a prince and are served dessert fit for a king.

Aunt Malika could have become famous if she had listened to my Father's advice. In his opinion, Faris should stop torturing himself and his customers with his restaurants. He should dress elegantly and concentrate on sales while his wife produced delectable sweets, cakes and other culinary treats. Aunt Malika laughed self-consciously.

As I mentioned, Uncle Faris did not particularly enjoy cooking; but he was nevertheless an expert on drinks of all kinds. He had his own still in the basement where he conjured up schnapps and other unusual, fragrant waters. Like many Damascenes, he produced his own rose, orange blossom and lemon blossom water.

It was in Damascus, more than a thousand years ago, that the art of distillation took its first steps and this is where alcohol was first produced through distillation. From the Damascene Rose (rosa damascena) they made the expensive attar of roses (essence) and rose water. They used the oil in medicine and for the production of perfumes. Rose water, though, is also an essential element in flavouring sweets and drinks in Damascus. Marzipan would be unthinkable without rose water.

Uncle Faris operated as hygienically as an apothecary. His still was famous throughout the neighbourhood, but he did not want to sell a single drop. He gave Mother a large bottle of orange blossom water every year. It was her favourite scent.

Sweets in Damascus are tremendously diverse, ranging from a large number of different candied fruits and sugar-coated nuts to colourful bonbons and similar specialities. Another big area is the special puff pastry and pasta dough products stuffed with pistachios, which belong amongst the most delicious of all Middle Eastern foods. They taste particularly dreamy in Damascus because Damascenes, unlike other Arabs or Turks, sweeten them only slightly rather than killing them with sugar syrup. It borders on magic the way the pistachios are held together so you can serve slices without a single pistachio falling out and yet it all still melts on the tongue.

Aunt Malika never makes such items herself. No one makes them at home because the ingredients are very expensive – pistachios, butter and sugar – and the end result is never as good as that of a renowned producer. There are shoddy versions, even in Damascus, but you can find at least ten decent speciality shops who offer these treats at a reasonable price.

Aunt Malika's strength lies elsewhere. She conjures up wonderful desserts in her kitchen. Sometimes she does it so easily and quickly that you have to ask yourself why you did not have the idea yourself.

٭ تمر وتين محشي ٭
Stuffed dates and figs

Preferably choose large dates with juicy flesh. Slit them open and remove the seed. Press peeled pistachios or roasted almonds into the middle and press the two halves together. You can also shape a small piece of marzipan like a seed and press it into the middle of the date.

For the figs, use dried ones, preferably as large and plump as possible. Remove the stem, open it up a bit from the bottom and push in a peeled walnut half and press the fig back together.

❋ You can also stuff the dates with sheep's cheese. They taste wonderful.

✻ معمول بالتمر أو الفستق ✻

Butter biscuits with date, fig or walnut stuffing

This is a very popular sweet that is on offer at practically every street corner in Damascus, though these are usually cheaply produced short-crust biscuits. They save on the butter. But not Aunt Malika. She only uses the best ingredients for her biscuits.

The biscuit dough

400 g finely ground durum wheat semolina
100 g wholewheat flour
500 g butter
3 tbsp rose water
200 ml water
1 tbsp dried yeast
200 g icing sugar (if desired)

Place the semolina in a large bowl and mix thoroughly with the flour. Soften the butter a bit, add it to the semolina-flour mixture and knead thoroughly. Add the rose water and mix again. Cover the dough and let it stand for 6 hours. Dissolve the yeast in 200 ml warm water and add to the dough, then knead for 10 minutes. The dough should be smooth and supple but not too runny. If necessary, add more semolina and flour. Leave the dough to rest 1 hour.

Date filling

250 g dates
150 g butter
1 tbsp rose water

Stone the dates and cut into small pieces. Preheat the butter in a pan over a low heat, add the dates and keep stirring until the dates and butter form a smooth mixture. Add the rosewater and allow the mixture to cool.

Pistachio filling

250 g pistachios
100 g granulated sugar
1 tbsp orange or lemon blossom essence

Peel the pistachios, chop finely and mix with the sugar. Then add the lemon or orange blossom essence, slightly diluted with water, and knead through again.

❁ Sometimes you can obtain rose, orange blossom, or lemon blossom water at Arab or Turkish grocers. If not, you can obtain the essence at delicatessens. But this essence is too concentrated and must be diluted a little before use.

Careful: never confuse orange blossom essence with orange peel essence! If neither should be available then rose water can be found in almost every chemist.

Walnut filling

250 g walnuts
100 g granulated sugar
1 tbsp rose water

Finely chop the walnuts and mix with the sugar and rosewater. Shape the dough into walnut sized balls and press a deep hole into the centre. Put ½ tsp filling in the hole and press the edges of the dough together over the filling.

Aunt Malika has various carved wooden moulds she dusts with flour and then lightly presses the dough into. The sharp edges of the mould pattern gave the surface a decorative look. Any pocket or any conical shaped mould is equally suitable for this. If you do not have a mould, you can draw lines with a fork across the surface of the dough without damaging it. Then place the balls of dough on a baking tray and allow to rest for half an hour. Then bake for 10 minutes in an oven preheated to 200° C/400° F/Gas Mark 6.

❋ You can also roll the dough out thinly and then cut rounds out using a large cup or a glass. Place the filling on half the rounds and use the remaining rounds to cover. Press the edges together. Lightly decorate the tops with a fork.

You can dust the baked biscuits with icing sugar, but that is a matter of preference. Many prefer this delicacy plain because the sugar can overwhelm many of the nuances of flavour.

Sugar syrup
500 g sugar
300 ml water
1 lemon
2 tsp orange blossom or rose water

Making sugar syrup is child's play. Dissolve the sugar in ca. 300 ml of water over low heat, skimming off foam if necessary. Add the lemon juice through a sieve and let cook another 10 minutes until the liquid has the consistency of runny honey. Let the syrup cool a bit and now add the rose water or the orange blossom (or lemon blossom) water. Stir vigorously and allow to cool.

❋ عش البلبل ❋

'Ush al bulbul
Nightingale nests

Damascenes are masters of the art of wrapping in every aspect.
Their pistachio rolls are famous. They are baked rolls with a
crisp coat of fine vermicelli that holds the pistachios together.
The roll is cut so precisely that not a single Pistachio falls out of
line. It borders on masochism to want to make these at home in
a normal household. Aunt Malika, though, has dug out an old
recipe that makes it relatively easy to make these in your own
kitchen. I have to admit I actually prefer her Nightingale Nests
because they are airier than the wonderful pistachio rolls from
a confectioner.

For this you need very thin, undamaged vermicelli (extremely
thin noodles), which you can obtain from Turkish or Arabic
grocers. In an airtight container they will keep up to a year in
the refrigerator.

500 g vermicelli (or lightly steamed noodles)
250 g butter
250 g salted pistachios
100 g granulated sugar
2 tbsp rose water
Sugar syrup

As a rule the noodles are a bit compressed and folded in their
vacuum packaging. Carefully unfold and loosen them. Soften
the butter over low heat. Add 100g of the butter to the noodles
and stir carefully until all the noodles are coated in butter.
Grease a baking tray with 50 g butter.

Peel the Pistachios and only use the best ones. Loosen the skins, which would taste bitter after baking, by rubbing a few of them at a time between your hands. Mix the Pistachios with the granulated sugar and rose water. Preheat the oven to 180° C/350° F/Gas Mark 4.

Twist or roll 5 to 7 noodles into little nests about the size of a walnut. Only the first ones are difficult. Once you discover the knack, the rest will form easily.

Set the nests close together on the tray. Melt the rest of the butter, ca. 100 g, and drizzle over the nests in a thin stream. Put the tray in the oven and bake until the noodles take on a light yellowish tone. Take the tray out, allow it to cool a bit and pore off the excess butter into a bowl.

Put 3 to 4 Pistachios in each nest. Return the tray to the oven until the nests turn light brown. Take them out of the oven, allow to cool a little, and drain off any excess butter. Then drizzle with the sugar syrup. Do not use too much syrup. You want the nests to remain dry and airy, and not dripping in syrup.

❊ You can vary the filling by using walnuts or peeled almonds instead of the Pistachios.

❊ كل وأشكر ❊

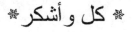

Kul'wa'shkur
Eat and praise

There are dishes whose name says it all. This cake is one of them.

500 g puff pastry
200 g pine nuts
200 g butterfat
50 g granular sugar

1 tbsp freshly ground cinnamon
1 tbsp orange blossom or rose water
Sugar syrup
50 g pistachios

Making your own puff pastry is time-consuming, but you can buy good, frozen puff pastry. Defrost it just before use. Fry the pine nuts to a golden yellow in the butterfat. Remove them from the pan immediately or they will go dark brown and bitter. Chop them up finely and mix together with the sugar, cinnamon and orange blossom or rose water.

Grease a 25 × 35 cm baking tin and put a layer of puff pastry in it overlapping the edge a bit. Carefully spread half the pine nut and sugar mixture on it and smooth it out. Place a second layer of pastry on top and then another layer of the remaining pistachio mixture. Smooth it out and cover with a last layer of puff pastry. Press down slightly with your hand all over.

Using a sharp knife, etch diamond shapes or squares into the surface so butter and syrup can seep through and the cake will be easier to cut later.

Brush the surface evenly with butter and bake 30 minutes in an oven preheated to 180° C/350° F/Gas Mark 4, until the surface is golden brown. Remove the cake from the oven, allow to cool a little, pour off excess butter and drizzle sugar syrup over it until it cannot absorb any more. Garnish the top with pistachios. Allow to cool to room temperature.

The cake tastes best when still slightly warm. Due to the high sugar content, the cake will keep at room temperature for several days if kept covered.

If you replace the pine nuts with pistachios or walnuts and leave out the cinnamon, this same recipe results in the best known Middle Eastern sweet in the world: baklava. It is

coveted from Greece to Saudi Arabia. Unfortunately, it is often
drowned rather than soaked in cheap sugar syrup so you taste
nothing but the heavy sweetness.

In contrast to their cooking of sweets, the Damascenes have surprisingly little to offer in the way of beverages. That Damascus is disappointingly unoriginal in this area is not a prejudice on the part of tourists; it is the sober truth. It does not surprise me that foreign refreshments are flooding the market. The lack of imagination in inventing drinks in such a hot country is all the more surprising since the water quality has always been good in Damascus. Or is the quality of the water itself the reason that it is found sufficiently refreshing?

Syria has never had good wines in its modern history. When you find out that the oldest known evidence for viniculture is a circa 8,000-year-old wine press with preserved grape seeds that was found in a burial mound of a prehistoric settlement south of Damascus, and given that the natural conditions are relatively good for wine-growing and could support the best grapes, what is on offer is all the more surprising and disappointing. The problem is that Damascus has not maintained a true wine tradition since the Arab conquest. Islam banned making wine under threat of punishment and although of course many Muslims drank – most typically the rulers who publicly condemned wine – everything happened secretly and depended on the good will of the local governor. If a strict fanatic was ruling, he did not shy from proscribing wine for the Christians and Jews, too, and sometimes even had the vines torn out of the ground. That would kill any tradition. The sweet wine is too heavy and the dry too sour.

First and foremost, Damascenes drink Arak, a highly alcoholic (up to 60 per cent by volume) grape-anise schnapps. It is drunk chilled and diluted with water. Production is costly, but Syrians and Lebanese are masters in 'cooking Arak'. It is made in two stages. First the alcohol is distilled from fermented grape juice. Then it is mixed with two thirds its volume of water and a fifth its weight of aniseeds, and then heated and held at temperature for 24 hours so the ethereal anise oils are drawn out by the alcohol. The speed, exact duration of distillation, quality of anise and grapes and not least storage conditions create the differences in quality of different variants of Arak.

Despite the fact that beer was invented in the Middle East, it almost disappeared completely from here and only returned by way of Europe. In the 1960s and 1970s, Middle Eastern beer was terrible. You could have drunk dishwater and it probably would not have tasted any nastier. The beer has improved with time, but it is still not good.

Tea, coffee, freshly squeezed fruit juices and modern refreshments are available everywhere. Uncle Faris has some old Damascene drink recipes. Many are not really possible to make because the starting ingredients require so much effort or are difficult to obtain. For example, there is a popular drink in Damascus made from liquorice, which is very refreshing chilled with ice cubes. But if you cannot pulverise the liquorice – and no domestic kitchen is equipped for that – then you cannot make this drink. However there are two drinks that can be made in any home and I have written them down here.

Airan

Yoghurt drink
½ l yoghurt
½ l water
½ tsp salt

Put the yoghurt in a bowl, then add salt and water. Whisk them together for about 5 minutes. Pour into a container and chill for 1 hour. Put a fresh mint leaf on the Airan when serving.

As a sendoff, Uncle Faris always makes coffee, for which our mother (who was herself famous for her coffee during her lifetime in our Abbara Alley) after her first sip expressed her respect with the words, *kahwet mu'allim*, supreme coffee.

No visit in Damascus, no matter how brief, is complete unless you have drunk coffee. It is drunk without, with some or with much sugar, but always with cardamom, which is added to the coffee either in whole pods or freshly ground. The Bedouins will often show the cardamom before adding it to the coffee to garner praise for its quality. The rounder and greener the pod, the better the cardamom. People in Damascus swear that coffee with cardamom after a meal has a miraculous effect on the digestion. That is why no meal is considered complete until coffee has been drunk.

Where the word coffee comes from cannot be determined with great certainty. It may originate in the Ethiopian word *Kaffa* (the name of a province in south-west Ethiopia where coffee was cultivated), but could also arise from the Arab word *Kahwa*, a term that used to be used to denote wine and all stimulating but appetite-curbing drinks. There is no dispute, by contrast, over the origin of the word mocha, which came from the Arab word *Mocha*, the name of the port city in the Yemen from which the coffee was delivered.

Who discovered coffee? Who boiled it for the first time? No one knows but legends abound. Supposedly a goatherd in Ethiopia, the original home of the coffee bean, noticed his goats were strangely agitated and behaved oddly when they ate from a particular plant.

In some places the story goes further. Shortly before Easter, the goatherd brings an abbot a kid, as he makes a gift to the monastery every year, in exchange for which the abbot blesses his herd. On this occasion the abbot complains to the shepherd that his monks have lately become so sleepy they have been missing evening prayers. The goatherd is supposed to have recommended to his fellow watcher over a flock that he give his monks the berries of this magical bush. He was certain they would become as lively as his goats.

In the Middle East, coffee tends to be viewed as an obligatory dessert after every meal. It is not, as in Europe or America, brewed in a large pot or jug, but boiled in small quantities over an open flame in long-handled little pots made of copper, brass or even aluminium.

Coffee begins a visit and ends it. It is served in small mocha cups. And by the way, coffee is never drunk with milk or cream.

In Damascus we distinguish between two types of coffee: the bitter and the sugared. The bitter, called *murra* or *sada*, is prepared from coarsely ground coffee and much cardamom and boiled for a long time. It is usually drunk on special occasions (weddings, funerals) and you take only a small sip of this bitter yet very aromatic concentrate. Sugared coffee, called *masbuta*, on the other hand is drunk in Damascus all the time and everywhere, including at Uncle Faris's.

❋ قهوة عربية ❋

Arabic Coffee

Per cup (mocha cup):
1 heaped tsp very finely ground Arabic coffee (if necessary,
Italian espresso will do)
1 tsp sugar or a bit less
1 small knife tip of freshly ground cardamom
A little more than a mocha cup of water

Bring the water to the boil in a long-handled little pot. Remove from the heat. Pour out enough of the water to fill a mocha cup and set aside. Add the coffee, sugar and cardamom to the pot and return to the heat. Carefully and with constant stirring bring it to the boil (it will foam incredibly).

As soon as the mixture has foamed three times, briefly remove it from the heat and add the cup of water you poured out earlier. Bring it to the boil one more time. Set it aside, covered with a small saucer for 1 minute, then serve.

Some women can read fortunes in the coffee grounds. Aunt Malika is one of the best coffee-ground-readers. You swirl the last sip – perhaps add a few grounds – and tip the cup on its side in the saucer. Then leave it to sit for five minutes. In the meantime, the dark grounds begin to paint bizarre landscapes on the inside wall of the cup. The 'reader' lets her eyes wander over these landscapes. She will repeatedly stop, gravely wrinkle her forehead, study the figures in detail, and often whisper meaningfully to a woman sitting next to her, 'Look at this gazelle here. Do you see the wolf behind it?' Frequently the woman will then say, 'Yes, yes,' even though she recognises neither gazelle nor wolf in the confusion ... or does she? It is like the shapes some people see in clouds and others do not recognise at all. Aunt Malika then tells of events in the future that the person who has drunk the coffee will experience. There is no reason to believe it all, but it is an excuse for a good laugh.

'Damascus is the Pearl of the Orient'

Roman Emperor Julian

Hammam, or
Of bathing in paradise

Right on the al Bzouriyya Spice Market stands one of the most beautiful of public baths: Hammam Nureddin (written out as *Nur al Din*, Light of the Faith). Nureddin is venerated by Damascenes as *al Shahid*, the Martyr, even though he actually died of a disease. Damascenes do this consciously to honour a man who not only fought against the Crusaders his entire life but also returned the city to a new renaissance after a long dark winter lasting over 400 years.

Until 750, Damascus was the capital of a global empire. But when the Abbasids captured power and chose Baghdad as their capital, Damascus was demoted to a provincial city. Antipathy toward rulers from Baghdad has sat deep in the souls of the people of Damascus ever since.

The long winter began with the Abbasids, then continued as the city was repeatedly conquered by rival various local rulers who plundered it, exploited it and allowed it to deteriorate. Nureddin, who liberated the city in 1154, introduced a period of greatness that lasted about 250 years until the destructive assault by the Mongols in 1400.

Nureddin was a strange yet brilliant persona, who was born at an inauspicious time but made the most of it. Arabia and Syria had splintered into small enemy states. The Crusaders had already been in Jerusalem for many years and had taken advantage of Arab disunity to expand their rule along the Mediterranean coast. Though the Crusaders never took Damascus, they repeatedly laid siege to it.

Nureddin was of Turkish extraction. His father had been governor of Aleppo and was the first to challenge the Crusaders in any noteworthy manner. Nureddin took over the reins when his father was assassinated and immediately recognised that the Crusaders' strength rested on the divisions between their opponents. Local Arab-Muslim rulers repeatedly allied themselves with the Crusaders in order to defeat an arch-enemy, usually another local ruler. Nureddin set out to unite Syria and from then on the Crusaders knew no peace. He soon reigned over a large contiguous empire that stretched from the Iraqi Mosul across the Lebanon, parts of Palestine to the south of Syria. As a next step, he sent his most dependable and capable war strategist to Egypt to bring that important country under his rule.

The man's name was *Asadaddin* (Lion of the Faith) and he was a Kurd. He easily conquered Egypt. After his death, his nephew took over Egypt and became the greatest fulfilment of all his Damascene master's dreams and plans. This nephew was an educated man who had accompanied his uncle to Egypt only reluctantly. Yet he turned out to be a great field commander and adroit diplomat. After Nureddin's death in 1174, he became the new ruler of Syria and Egypt. His name was *Salahaddin* (Loving Kindness of the Faith). The Europeans call him Saladin out of sheer laziness.

As far as Nureddin is concerned, he too was far more than a field commander. He concerned himself as much with the development of Damascus and it seems as though he had selected Damascus to be the capital of his great empire, before his death in 1174 prevented him from realising his plan. Nevertheless during the barely 20 years he spent in Damascus the city must have been one single gigantic construction site. He built schools, mosques, baths and the first modern hospital (Maristan Nureddin) in the world. The hospital is not far from the Al Bzouriyya Spice Market. It was divided into different departments: surgery, orthopaedics, fever diseases and mental illness. When a patient arrived, he was examined in the carpeted reception (*Iwan*) and then referred to the relevant department where he would be taken care of by doctors. If he required inpatient treatment, he would be sent to one of the rooms to be given medicine and looked after. Every day the senior consultant would visit, accompanied by a nurse who wrote down everything the doctor had to say about the patient and then followed his instructions. Each patient had a chart in which what he was given in nourishment and medication was recorded.

There are many legends about this hospital, in which also music was used successfully for the first time to treat the soul.

In order to underwrite the free treatment of patients and the salaries of the medical staff the hospital was assigned vast estates, from which it could collect rents.

The hospital was still functioning perfectly even in the 16th century, as reported by the famous traveller Ibn Jubair. Today, after a thorough renovation, the Maristan Nureddin with its famous red dome is a Museum for Medicine and Science.

In contrast, the Hammam, which also carries Nureddin's name and was built by him in 1171, had fallen into decay by 1500, was renovated around 1600, deteriorated again and was even used as a warehouse until the city administration rediscovered this jewel of oriental architecture. They bought it, lovingly restored it in line with old records and returned it to its original intended purpose. It is now the most famous hammam in Damascus.

The only thing bathing in a hammam has in common with bathing in private at home is the end result – coming out clean. Going to the hammam is a social occasion, which is why Damascenes rarely go there alone. You bathe amongst familiar faces.

Most of the public baths in Damascus are magnificent structures. Some exceed the beauty of the mosques and churches. The comparison to the houses of God is not excessive. Damascenes, and in this they are Arabian, have an almost religious regard for water. They feel good when they are near it. The desert is in every Arab and he is as happy as a rescued child when he hears water splashing about. Islam requires that the believer wash as a precondition for the cleansing of the soul, without which prayer is not valid and will not be heard. You wash your face, hands and feet (the lesser ablution) in the inner courtyard of the mosque – which all have to have running water – before you enter the prayer hall. In the event of greater pollution, a thorough bath (greater ablution) is mandatory.

Unlike Christianity, Islam does not abhor the human body as the site of 'original sin'. Rather it elevates it as the second half of the soul. The ablutions cleanse both body and soul.

Damascenes do not go to the hammam in order to be finished quickly, but to linger, relax and relish the calm, hear and spread tales, rumours and gossip, get a massage, and then, exhausted and wrapped in soft, snow white towels slurp a hot tea next to the splish-splashing basin in the entrance hall. This is the forecourt of paradise for a Damascene.

It is no surprise that Damascenes call out, *Na'iman!*, be happy, to someone who has just come from a hammam. Na'iman also means living well, gently or peacefully. All this, the Damascenes believe, points to one thing: Paradise.

That is why it was the custom in Damascus that you even invited your guests to the hammam, to grant them this pleasure.

Damascus has an ancient tradition of public baths. The Romans appreciated the baths of the city and elaborated them into ostentatious palaces. When the Arabs, coming out of the desert, conquered Damascus, they cared for the baths with the soul of one who has fallen in love. The baths of Damascus became proverbial. Caliph al Walid ben Abdulmalik said to the Damascenes prior to beginning his massive building project, 'You are right to take pride in four rarities – your water, your air, your fruit and your hammams. I want to give you a fifth one – the Umayyad Mosque.'

Hammam culture was truly appreciated in Damascus and the number of baths rose steadily. By the 12th century there were over 112 baths. But with the coming of the modern era, interest in this pleasure declined. Modern architects responded to the hectic pace of the new era, which even Damascus had not avoided. They planned for a shower stall or bath in every house. By 1940, there were only 62 public baths, by 1950 a modest 29 and by 1975 only 10.

The façade of a hammam gives little away. Sometimes it looks like the entry to a normal block of flats, except that its domed roof resembles a mosque. The many cupolas have beautiful harmonious patterns of round blue windows. Damascenes lovingly refer to these little windows as *Qaimariyya*. *Qaimar* means moon, so they mean that these little windows allow in soft light like the moon. They allow this light into the interior of the bath without enabling voyeurs to peer in.

The hammam contains three areas, defined by their proximity to or distance from the outside world: *barrani* (the outer), *wastani* (the middle) and *juani* (the inner). The farther in you go, the more the temperature increases. There are many tiny details that differentiate one bath from another, but this tripartite division is a constant.

The first (outer) area, barrani, resembles the inner courtyard of an elegant house with a fountain, benches, mirrors, a dome, ceiling lights and colourful windows. This is where guests enter and are prepared for their bath. This is also where bathers return to enjoy the last tranquil moments before they dress and take their leave. And this is where the proprietor or bath master sits and directs his staff. For reasons of hygiene, everyone, guests as well as employees, wears wooden shoes with leather buckles, called *qabqab*. Street shoes are handed in to be looked after at the entrance.

In the middle (wastani) and inner (juani) areas there are no windows so that none of the heat is wasted. During the day, light enters through the aforementioned tiny panes in the domes of the ceiling, and at night there is artificial lighting. Wastani and juani are rooms in which you bathe. Hot and cold water flows into basins of stone or marble. The floor is usually made of marble and colourful, dressed stone.

The heating system is cleverly designed and allows very little heat to escape. The boiler room is under the hammam and always near the juani, the inner area. In order to avoid any dirt, the boiler room can only be accessed from the outside. It lies about four metres underground. There are two massive copper boilers over the firebox. The boiler man lets cold water flow into the first one and brings it close to the boil. He then transfers the hot water to the second boiler through a large pipe. This second boiler is always kept warm. He continually refills the first boiler with cold water. Hot water pipes run from the second boiler under the floors to the basins. The hot smoke of the fire is not sent up the chimney without having first spent its heat under the flooring of the hammam. That is why the flooring in the middle and inner chambers is always warm or even hot. Every hammam also has a cistern in the event that there is an interruption in the water supply.

When he enters the hammam, the bather is greeted by a bath master (women are greeted by a bath mistress) and given a seat and the wooden shoes he must wear while in the building. Then the master calls for an apprentice or messenger boy who hurries to the guest and lays a large cloth on the floor in which his clothes will be kept safe. Then he holds up another towel, like a folding screen, so the guest can disrobe without being looked at by others (or perhaps in order not to present a disturbing spectacle to the others). As soon as the bather is naked, the lad elegantly wraps the towel around his belly and legs and tucks the corner in so adroitly that it will not come loose. Then he takes the bundle of clothes to the master at the till for safekeeping. The guest personally hands over any valuables (wallet, watch, jewellery, etc) to the master.

Now the guest moves into the middle part of the bath, wastani, in which the light from the little blue windows in the dome exudes a strange calm. A second member of staff greets him at the entrance and asks him whether he wants any hair removed. If yes, he leads him to a special chamber and hands him a special cream designed for that purpose. If not, he asks whether he requires soap and sponge and whether he would like the services of an assistant (in the hammam he is called a soaper or scrubber) for washing. Some like to wash alone; others are happy to have a soaper wash them thoroughly. Finally the member of staff inquires whether the guest would like a massage after his bath. When he has heard everything the guest desires, he leaves. If the soaper (sometimes a hammam has several) happens to be occupied at that moment, then the member of staff returns to the guest and leads him into the inner chamber where you can hardly see for all the steam. The assistant seats the guest on a bench that is directly over the furnace. He sprays water on the hot floor so the guest sits and sweats. You can remain in this sauna of sorts for as long as you like. Eventually the man returns with a copper tub. He fills it with warm water. The guest is to relax and soak his feet in it.

If the bather now wants to go to the soaper and he is available, he returns to the middle area. He is led into one of the special side chambers that usually surround the middle hall, where he gets a friendly reception from the soaper. The guest sits on the warm floor, which usually has lovely designs made from marble, basalt and granite. He keeps the protective towel on the entire time. Walking around naked in a bath is deeply frowned on in Damascus. The soaper squats in front of the guest. He pulls a little woollen sack over his hand and shows it to the guest to confirm it cleanliness. He soaps the sack, takes the guest's right hand and begins to rub it with the sack, until after a while, with something like pride, he shows the guest how much dirt and dead skin he has managed to remove. Then he moves on to the right arm, the left hand and then the left arm. Next the guest has to lie down on his back. With lightening speed the assistant appears with a folded towel that he pushes under the guest's head like a pillow. Now face, chest and legs are soaped and rubbed down. The soaper repeatedly shows the guest how dirty the little sack has become, before soaping it up again and continuing to rub.

This scrubbing can hurt unbelievably sometimes. Damascenes used to call these chambers *maslach*, abattoirs, because people would emerge from these agonizing enjoyable tortures with reddened skin. Following this treatment the guest's hair is washed as often as necessary to make it 'squeak'. Then the guest is rinsed with warm water.

The whole process is repeated once again with new soap and a new sponge (usually a loofah or piece of hemp fabric) and when the soaper is finished he gently taps the guest on the back and says 'Na'iman' to him.

If the guest still has the strength and desires it, he is now massaged in another room. Massage has nothing to do with eroticism or gentleness here. It is more likely to resemble freestyle wrestling. Afterwards the guest has forgotten his fatigue and is simply grateful he is still alive.

Whether with or without massage, he returns to the inner chamber after washing and sweats for a while and douses himself with water. Then he slowly returns to the middle hall, sits down and douses himself with water again. You do this as slowly as you possibly can, as the point is to acclimatise yourself to the cooler temperatures. Finally the guest gives a nod to the assistant that he wants to go. He comes with dry, clean towels, wraps the guest's stomach, back, shoulders and head and leads him into the outer chamber, where he thoroughly rubs him down until he is truly dry. The guest is once again wrapped in fine towels and takes a seat on a bench. He sits there, thoroughly kneaded and swathed, converses with other guests, drinks tea or coffee and listens to the garrulous babbling of the fountain.

The guest is thoroughly rubbed down and dried off one more time before his clothing is returned to him.

Once dressed he goes to the bath master, pays and leaves a gratuity for all the assistants and then exits the hammam.

As a rule there are specific times or days for men and women. On the days for men, there is only tea and, for all the relaxation, the atmosphere is hushed and serious. It is quite different with the women. It is as though they wait to cross the threshold before throwing off the weight of the world. From the moment they greet each other they are being merry and making jokes. They bring cooked foods, pickled foods, snacks, watermelons, oranges, walnuts, raisins and pistachios. All of a sudden, the bath takes on the appearance of an outing. Sometimes you can hear the women's laughter all the way out in the street.

In the old days, women removed all their unwanted hair with a cream made from quicklime and arsenic, but this was banned in Damascus after several men died of arsenic poisoning. These days, harmless creams or razors are used.

Many mothers have met their future daughter-in-law in the hammam. This is where young women are introduced to the facts of life. Boys are allowed into the hammam with their mothers on women's days as long as they remain 'innocent'. Depending on the child, the age cut off lies between seven and nine years of age. This is where the boys have their first experiences with women. They play naturally and intimately with the girls.

The mistress keeps watch with an eagle eye that no older boy finagles his way in because that causes trouble amongst the women. Bad luck to the boys who are big for their age. They are assumed to be older than they are and no amount of oath swearing on the part of the disappointed mother will help. The boy has to return home.

Should a not-so-naive boy slip through the control then he will be able to hide his interest in the opposite sex at best once. The women will suggest to the mother, initially in code and jokingly, that her son is no longer a child. 'My goodness, how lovely the young man is. He should marry soon.' 'How old is your blest son?' 'Next time you can bring his father along, as well.'

As a rule the women make their point with humour. But if, as can happen, a mother, for whatever reason, insists on bringing her son along, then the other women will step up their attack. You can guarantee that the boy will not come back a second time because the mistress will remember the woman and her son. The stricter the mistress is, the more popular the bath, because the women want to keep their secrets to themselves and have greater fear of the tittle-tattle of self-aware boys than for their own chastity.

Two splendid examples of Damascene architecture surround the Hammam Nureddin and strangely enough the same man, the unfortunate Governor As'ad Pasha al-Azem, planned them both.

A few steps back on the same side as the hammam is Khan al-Azem. The word khan is often translated as caravanserai. It sounds nicer than khan (pronounced khaan), but it is incorrect. Caravanserais were protected stops on the long trade routes, modest but well-fortified structures in which caravans could rest and restock their provisions.

The word *khan* comes from the Persian and means house. A khan is a large, beautiful building, which served as a point of arrival for the traders.

Here they could stay the night and trade, and have their animals looked after.

Unlike in a caravanserai, the city's largest merchants had permanent offices in the khan, where they traded in spices, cloth, grain, seeds, precious metals and precious woods amongst others. Some khans are more reminiscent of a cathedral than of a sober house of trade. In this, one of the most beautiful khans, As'ad Pasha esnsured his name would be immortalised. When the French poet and politician Alphonse de Lamartine travelled to Damascus and the Middle East in 1832, he was amazed by the khan: 'A people, whose architects have the capability to design such a khan and whose builders are able to master its construction, is a great people and full of life.'

A few hundred metres farther along, set back a bit, is the second memorial to the unfortunate governor.

The Azem Palace, Arabic *Kasr al-Azem*, is a key sight in any tourist guide. Governor As'ad Pasha al-Azem built the stateliest house of the city in 1749. He was the son of a governor and had practiced administering cities for the sultan in Istanbul, before he eventually took over Damascus. He was a clever, ambitious politician and from 1743 to 1756 he ruled Damascus with an iron fist in the name of the Ottoman sultan. But As'ad Pasha had ambitions to rule over a far greater dominion than a city. The sultan in Istanbul was not pleased. He first transferred him from Damascus to Aleppo, and then later, after there was unrest in the south supposedly instigated by the ex-governor, the sultan invited As'ad Pasha for a talk. He was sufficiently experienced to be suspicious of this invitation, but it did offer him an opportunity to clarify matters with the Sultan and thus triumph over his archrival.

As'ad Pasha delayed his departure. But when the Sultan sent him a letter guaranteeing his safety (Arabic *Aman*, a document in which the sultan warrants he will protect a person's blood and not squander a drop of it and which in the language of the time meant absolute security), he agreed to go.

As'ad Pasha al-Azem went on his journey, but before he met the sultan he was strangled in a bath (in other versions, in a library). He was just 56 years of age. In strangling him, the professional killers took every care not to break the word of the sultan.

Shortly afterwards, the sultan confiscated the governor's possessions.

The governor seems to have been haunted by premonitions of his premature demise during the building of Damascus's most famous palace. He was in such a hurry that he recruited workmen, master builders, planners, calligraphers, marble masons, carpenters and construction workers from the whole country and had them work around the clock. The entire country suffered: other projects lay idle because neither building materials nor workmen were to be found. His urgency had other unfortunate effects. The Pasha frequently had columns, tiles, beams and other valuable pieces taken out of mosques, historic buildings and houses of noble Damascenes. The haste with which his demolition crew replaced appropriated beams with temporary support led to the collapse of many of those structures.

There is no doubt this building is a feast for the eyes, but its beauty disguises much suffering, not least that of its builder.

The Wit and Wisdom of Damascus

The Damascene dialect has given us a welter of popular sayings that are pithy, earthy, short and sweet and have a music all their own.

Sayings are the philosophy of the ordinary man or woman in the street, and offer us an insight into their innermost psyche. For all their pithiness, they have running through them a common thread that guides us through the labyrinthine twists and turns of the Damascene soul, laying bare its strengths and weaknesses and its core moral values. Sayings are coined by individuals who remain forever anonymous.

On the other hand, they can sometimes show their age – it's not uncommon for some nugget of wisdom that must have seemed profound in its time to appear anachronistic or even reactionary to us nowadays. Some sayings also encapsulate centuries of oppression and subservience. A good example of this is the phrase *I call the man who marries my mother 'Uncle'*. Rather than saying anything about the happiness or misfortune of the widowed mother, all this conveys is the son's resigned acceptance. Likewise, there are sayings that capture the whole mindset of the despot, such as *Starve your dog and he'll follow you obediently*. Of course, for 'dog', read 'subject' here.

That said, the treasure chest of Damascus sayings contains some real gems that are a joy to the ear.

On kindness: Give me a friendly greeting and I'll happily go without food.

On patience: Patience is the key to relief.

On mutability: When a guest arrives, he's a prince; as soon as he's sat down, he's his host's prisoner.

On close friends: You've got many brothers who didn't come from your mother's womb.

On presumption: Whenever a thoroughbred horse gets shod, there's a cockroach waving his legs around shouting 'I'm next!'.

On being a loudmouth: If a loud voice was worth anything, the ass would be king of the animals.

On decisiveness: You can't hold two watermelons in one hand.

On being envied: Keeping a straight course confuses your enemies.

On looking after things: Anyone who doesn't cherish old things doesn't deserve anything new.

On neighbours: Before you move into a new house, check out the neighbours.

On child-rearing: When your children are small, educate them; when they're grown-up, make them your friends.

On healing: Talking with a friend cleanses your heart.

On stupidity: It's easier to empty the sea with a mussel shell than it is to rid someone of their stupidity.

On the relativity of beauty: To his parents, a monkey is prettier than a gazelle.

On humility: Don't stretch your feet out beyond your mattress.

On an unlucky person: When he started dealing in coffins, suddenly no-one wanted to die any more.

On vanity: On his way to the gallows, the vain person said: 'I hope the noose goes with my suit'.

On fear: If you're afraid, keep quiet, and if you speak out, have no fear.

On false friends: A friendship between a cat and a mouse brings ruin to a house.

Arrested time, or
Of coffee houses and monumental structures

Stand in the Al Bzouriyya Spice Market, and you are in the middle of the historically most important part of the Old City. There is so much in a small space of 600 by 700 metres that it would take several pages just to list it all. Everything that belongs to a classic Arabian city is here: the largest mosque, the market, the many hammams, the showy houses of influential patricians, the khans, schools and hospitals. This was once the seat of power. Caliphs, sultans and governors lived in this area, but also poets and philosophers who changed the world. In the seventh century, Damascus was the capital of a global empire. Not without reason are the most impressive examples of Arab-Islamic architecture here for all to admire, including the Citadel that Saladin inhabited. The centrepiece of all these buildings steeped in history is the Umayyad Mosque.

This massive mosque (approximately 100 by 150 metres in size) was once the largest in the world. To this day it is considered the fourth holiest shrine after the mosques in Mecca, Medina and Jerusalem. Before the mosque was built, there was a much larger temple, 300 by 380 metres in size, on a hill above the city, built by the Aramaians and dedicated to their weather god, Hadad. The Romans supplanted Hadad and put Jupiter in his stead. In the fourth century, under Emperor Theodosius, a basilica dedicated to John the Baptist replaced the temple. Legend has it that, after his decapitation, John's supporters brought his head from present-day Palestine to Damascus for safekeeping.

When the Arabs conquered Damascus in 635 and drove out the Romans, they allowed the churches to remain. For 70 years, they used St John's Church alongside Christians as a house of god, the first time in history that conquerors had been so generous as to pray in the church of the defeated. Christians used the western part of the church and Muslims used the eastern part. It was only under Caliph al Walid bin Abd al Malik, a man not particularly fond of Christians, that the entire structure was converted into a magnificent mosque. He valued state power more than tolerance and peace treaties. No amount of protest helped the Christians. Much later his successor transferred title of some estates to the Christians in exchange for the confiscated property, and they were satisfied with this.

Al Walid wanted to create the most beautiful mosque in the world. It took him seven (in some narratives, ten) years and all of Syria's tax receipts. He had artists come from Constantinople, Persia and India, and rewarded them handsomely. To this day, the influence of Byzantine art is visible in the representations of a paradisiacal landscape at the main entrance to the prayer hall, which, as a piece of representational art, is an exception in the Islamic world. By contrast, the repetition of drawings, geometric shapes and structural components (such as columns or arches) is pure Arab, while the vivid, luminous colours and the lavish precision of the complicated intertwining of plants and scripts are Persian. In the Umayyad Mosque, the influences of many significant cultures of the past blend together to form a fascinating new whole.

The mosque was built with peerless opulence. Gold and precious stones adorned the walls, lavish arabesques and mosaic pictures covered the floors and ceilings. The Umayyad Mosque was also the first to have a minaret, from the Arabic *manarat*, a lighthouse. The mosque has three minarets, the most important being the one in the East, the Jesus Minaret. Muslims firmly believe that, when the world ends, Jesus Christ will return from heaven to earth by way of this minaret to fight against the false messiah.

Today the mosque – like much else in Damascus – offers only a faint semblance of its earlier magnificence. There have been over ten great fires since its first construction, some of which were so bad that only the massive stone structure of the building was left. On some occasions, earthquakes and wars have demolished what only just been restored. But again and again Damascenes have restored their mosque with patience and love.

One curiosity in departing: On the left in the prayer hall is a lovingly tended and richly decorated shrine. It is the grave of John the Baptist whom Muslims worship as *Yahja* (Arabic, he lives) and as one of the prophets who preceded Muhammad.

The mosque has four gates. If you go out of the Northern Gate and then bear westwards you will come to Saladin's Mausoleum.

Saladin, who in Europe is mentioned in the same breath as Richard the Lion Heart and the Crusades, and who has the reputation worldwide of being a wise victor, is considered a hero in Damascus and a symbol of courage and not giving up, no matter how hopeless the situation. Arabs also like to use him as an example of how prisoners are supposedly treated in Arabia. Stories are told of his generosity to the defeated, which prefer to conceal, however, that he was a Kurd. They also tend to avoid mention of his complex personality for fear Saladin's heroic image might be sullied. It is undisputed that he was a genius as a field commander and diplomat. But he was also an extremely fanatical Sunni and as such was more likely to be merciless toward Shiites, Ismailites and other Muslim sects than toward Crusaders.

Arabs also like to overemphasise the fact that he only owned a few coins. This fact is in all the school textbooks, but of course Saladin had little need for small change. He owned everything. He divided up his empire, which stretched from Egypt to northern Syria, amongst his sons and brothers as if he were dividing up his own private farm.

In actuality, the fear that his heroic image might be damaged is totally unfounded because what he gave the Arabs, and especially the Syrians and Egyptians, borders on a miracle.

Saladin's Mausoleum lies at the northwest corner of the mosque and was built in 1195. The domed building contains two sarcophagi. Kaiser Wilhelm II donated the sarcophagus on the left in 1898 during his aforementioned visit to Damascus. The German Kaiser had three motives for this conciliatory act: it was certainly a friendly gesture toward the Arabs, it was a show of respect for Saladin, the great military strategist; and it was an attempt to improve diplomatic relations with the Ottoman sultan in order to strengthen German influence in the Middle East. Damascenes particularly value how the Kaiser behaved, because the memory of an insult by another European is burned in their brains.

When, after the insurgent Arabs had suffered heavy losses to shake off Ottoman rule, the French and British then divided up the Middle East behind their backs, the Syrians rebelled. A small group, clumsy but courageous, gathered and confronted the French army that was rolling toward Damascus. Some, as a very old neighbour told us 40 years ago, were seeing a tank for the first time in their lives. They attacked with sticks, stones and knives and were mown down by cowardly machine guns and tanks. The battle at Maisalun near Damascus did not last long. The field commander, General Gouraud, marched into Damascus, and, still wearing his battle uniform, went to Saladin's Mausoleum to scream, almost hysterically, at the dead in the grave: 'Saladin, we have returned. My presence seals the triumph of the cross over the crescent.'

But after bitter resistance and over 25 years of occupation, the French had to withdraw again. Saladin is still here.

Two curiosities as an aside: One: the generosity of the Germans has inadvertently preserved their ignorance in marble. They donated the sarcophagus not realising that Muslims never rebury their dead. To this day it stands empty next to the real one from the 12th century.

Two: the German Kaiser also laid with great ceremony a large bronze laurel wreath he had brought from Berlin on the grave of the Arab commander. But when T E Lawrence, better known as Lawrence of Arabia – an agent of the British Secret Service and organiser of the Arab Revolt against the Ottomans – marched into Damascus in 1918 and discovered the bronze wreath with the name of the German Kaiser, he seized it as war booty because the Germans and their Ottoman allies had lost the First World War. He sent it to London.

But back to the Umayyad Mosque. If you go out of the Western Gate (also known as *Bab al-Barid*, Post Gate), just a few metres away you see the gigantic, almost 10-metre-high columns that belonged to the western gate of the Jupiter Temple, the rest of which has long since been buried under the rubble of the city. There is also a small centuries-old book and school supplies market here and a few paces farther along is the eastern entrance to the large roofed Souq al Hamidiyya, one of the best-known markets of Damascus.

Do you remember the ice cream shop, Bakdash? It still exists and is as famous as ever. There you see the priest next to the Bedouin, the work-man next to the teacher, and tourists next to a high-ranking officer. Elbow to elbow they sit at long tables, and, just as in the old days, they serve that vanilla ice cream that strong men beat with mashers in large chilled vats until it becomes creamy and smooth – Bakdash's classic dish, which no machine can reproduce.

At the end of the Souq is the famous Citadel of Damascus, which was a prison for many years. Today it is a tourist attraction, but it is modest when compared to the Citadel of Aleppo. The new city of Damascus starts beyond the al Hamidiyya Souq. It probably harbours remains of old settlements, mosques and schools here and there, but most of it is relatively modern and looks like all modern cities. So let us go back to our trusty Old City and the Umayyad Mosque.

The Southern Gate of the mosque, which is behind the prayer niches, is frequently closed because entry through here would disturb those pray-ing. That is why the city administration has designated the Northern, and at times Western, Gate as the entrance for tourists.

The Southern Gate leads to the once large Goldsmiths' Souq, of which, since a devastating fire in 1960, only fragments remain. From here it is only a few steps back to the Spice Market.

If you stand in the great courtyard of the mosque, so that the prayer hall is on your right, you can see the Eastern Gate and just to the right of the corner of the wall, the famous Jesus Minaret. The Eastern Gate leads to Naufara Street by way of some steps. On the right is the famous coffee house with its even more famous storyteller, Arabic *Hakawati*, who tells his listeners exciting tales night after night.

But before we go in, we should probably explain a little bit about the history of coffee houses. The first coffee house in the world was probably opened in Damascus in 1530. It was named Rose Café. Two Syrians opened the first coffee house in Istanbul in 1574. The coffee house, then called *Kahwekhane*, soon became a meeting place for intellectuals, where they played backgammon and listened to poets performing their work. Not long after, coffee houses began to open on every corner. Strict Islamic scholars thought this new fashion to be competition for the mosque and even went so far as to consider the coffee house even more diabolical than wine houses. The Muftis did not stop campaigning against the coffee houses until Sultan Murad III (1574–1595) had all coffee houses closed – after someone also informed him that politics was being discussed in these establishments and his rule was being criticised. The prohibition lasted a long time. It was only toward the end of the rule of Mehmet IV (1648–1687) that the sale of coffee was once again allowed, and coffee houses began to open their doors in the many capitals of the Ottoman Empire.

Coffee houses have undergone great and complicated changes. Initially they were the reserve of the upper classes, but over time they became accessible to every one. They remain, however, the exclusive domain of men. In the Christian Quarter of Damascus, some premises, particularly those with outside tables, are called *Kahwet 'A'ilat*, Family Café, but the name is deceptive. These are not coffee houses, they are restaurants.

Arab cafés were never and are still not comfortable. In many cases they are also hideously decorated. Naked light bulbs dangle from the ceiling or they have the even uglier neon tubes, which are more likely to remind you of a hospital or customs office than beautiful Damascus. Yet the cafés are full night after night. They are thick with smoke and yet the men squeeze together on wooden benches and antediluvian chairs to quietly smoke their hookah, drink coffee and tea and listen to the Hakawati, the coffee house storyteller.

As Damascus has not known freedom of expression for over 500 years and the official news is more likely to be lies then the truth, the café plays a decisive role in how the public gets its news.

But let us go inside now.

The people here are as colourful as Damascus itself: young students in casual jeans, office workers in suits, and more mature men in traditional garb. The coffee house storyteller seems to be immune to radio and television. He fascinates young and old equally. Strangely enough, he has to disguise himself. He puts a red Turkish fez, Arabic *tarbush*, on his head, like the city dwellers used to wear in the previous century, throws on the traditional Bedouin black cloak, Arabic *abaya*, and takes a ridiculous sword in his right hand. He could not dress himself in a more comical and contradictory manner. Apparently he does this for the tourists, as you see them amongst the guests again and again.

He speaks loudly to make himself heard over the noise. People listen intently and laugh. Every once in a while he will bang his sword on the table to shake awake those who have become sleepy.

How often have people fought in this room, because some were on the side of the hero and the others found the character that was meant to be the enemy sympathetic? Comments from the audience, clapping or fighting leave the coffee house storyteller unmoved. It's all part of people identifying with the characters.

At first the storyteller has to compete against the noise and apparent inattention. But the more suspenseful the story becomes, the quieter the audience grows. At the tensest point the storyteller will interrupt his tale, say when the hero is thrown in jail, or is about to be executed, or is being chased or is simply hanging from his beloved's balcony by his fingertips – the raconteur does not neglect to mention of course that it was a wet and stormy night. Who would be surprised that some listeners have difficulty falling asleep later that night, go to the storyteller, wake him and sometimes threaten him or offer him money to hear the rest of the tale so they can sleep peacefully? The storyteller will do this under one condition: that the intruders still come to the café the next day. After all, he earns his money on a per listener basis. And he does not earn badly. That is why every coffeehouse storyteller makes an effort to be more thrilling than his competition. Although his stories may be exaggerated, theatrical or even shallow, the Hakawati is the undisputed master in one thing: he knows precisely how to begin a story and when and how he must interrupt or end it.

For a time it seemed that television had virtually wiped out the storytellers, but the tradition of the Hakawati seems to be experiencing a renaissance.

The coffeehouse at the Umayyad Mosque used to be famous for a special tea ceremony, which has become unthinkable in today's rush. Our father was very fond of this ceremony and tried to replicate this artful pouring of tea at home with some success. All over the Middle East, as is well known, tea is drunk from small delicate glasses and has been cooked in a type of samovar for hundreds of years. Basically there are two pots, one containing a very concentrated tea, the other boiling water, which are placed one on top of the other, so that the upper teapot is always kept warm by the steam from what essentially becomes a double boiler.

In the coffeehouse at the Umayyad Mosque they took advantage of the peculiarities of liquids caused by surface tension, though they had little precise knowledge of the laws of physics behind it. The pourers empirically discovered that surface tension depends on the density and temperature of a fluid. If you pour water into the glass first and then gently pour in the strong tea down the side of the glass, it will form a separate layer over the water. The result looks great and the guest then adds a little spoon of sugar and finally stirs the two liquids together. True masters can even achieve three layers: water, tea, water. Those were the little joys of everyday life.

When you come out of the café and continue along Naufara Street, you reach the Qaimarriyeh Quarter, at the beginning of which the remains of the Jupiter Temple are still visible. In the 19th century this Quarter was the throbbing heart of Damascene craft trades. Here there were silk-weaving mills, wood- and metal-working businesses, print works, factories producing food and sweets, marquetry workshops and tanneries. The Quarter was known as Little India. It's quiet here nowadays, and a pleasant place to live. A direct path leads from this quarter to Bab Sharqi and Bab Touma, where we started our tour. But before we end our walk, we are going to visit Uncle Farid, who lives not 300 metres from Naufara Street. A fireworks display awaits us there to wish us farewell.

Fireworks, or
How Uncle Farid tempts us into conversation

Uncle Farid is an unusual man. He loves and admires his wife so much that it confuses many of his male relations and friends. They like him for his unbelievable hospitality, but in secret they think he is an odd chap. For a long time they tried to make him look ridiculous and to convince their wives that his wife, Afifa, rather than he, was the man of the house. She held the sceptre in her hand. He was only so affectionate because he was afraid of her. Everyone would see that, when it really counted, he was not a real man. Comments such as these are the last weapon many men will use against someone who respects his wife. They cannot imagine masculinity and respect for women co-existing.

But when it really did count, all of these men ducked and pretended to be deaf, dumb and blind. A sadist moved into the area – an informer for the secret service. All of a sudden he was in their midst. He humiliated the men, insulted the women and tormented the children of the neighbourhood. The men prayed with their wives to Mother Mary that she would bless this awful man with the pox and bone cancer, preferably combined with the loss of his limbs.

But the blessed virgin was busy with other matters and so did not respond. The men cowered. No one wanted to be the first to be made an example of. Only Uncle Farid did not duck. When he saw one day how the secret agent shouted at a girl offensively, he went to call on him for an hour. The neighbours soon heard the informer groaning and begging for mercy. Uncle Farid eventually came out smiling and said to the neighbours who were standing around the courtyard with gaping mouths: 'That man will not be doing anything from now on.'

And indeed, the man did nothing until he moved out of the alley. Even when the children intentionally kicked a ball at him, he only smiled self-consciously and joked around with them to cover his embarrassment.

What Uncle Farid did and how he did it, he would never say. So then the men said: 'Yes, Uncle Farid is quite brave, but he is still not a real man.' But the men who said that were being foolish, because they had no idea how openly the women of Damascus talked with one another. When the women of the neighbourhood and relations of Aunt Afifa found out what a wonderful lover her husband was, they forbade all nasty comments about Uncle Farid's masculinity. So what other choice did the men have but to declare him as odd or crazy?

Besides, everyone, woman or man, likes Uncle Farid for his hospitality. And in this he is truly special. The relatives refer to him only as 'our Bedouin', because he is as generous as the legendary Bedouins. Just like a Bedouin, he feeds his guests as though they were just short of starving. But his guests are not hungry; he is. Uncle Farid is hungry for conversation, for storytelling. After a tale is told successfully he will often say: 'It was worth cooking for two days for that alone.'

His visitors are aware of that and so save all their quirky stories for him. I do the same, to return one joy for the thousand this splendid man has given us.

Uncle Farid is a good listener. He savours it when someone tells him a tale. He does not talk much himself, but he creates the atmosphere that seems to draw out stories as if of their own accord.

He is a traffic policeman and earns little, but he supplements his income with the many gifts motor vehicle drivers send him. He has exemplary control over his district.

Twice already the Minister for Transport has given him the award for 'Best Policeman of the Year'. Pedestrians, deliverymen and residents always know that if there is a problem, Uncle Farid has a solution. That is why he comes home laden with delicious titbits every day.

As soon as he enters the little house his wife inherited from her parents, he exchanges his uniform for a comfortable leisure suit and waters the flowers and plants in the inner courtyard, where the floor is covered with beautiful multicoloured tiles. Soon everything is glistening and shining with freshness. Then he quickly drinks a mocha and starts cooking.

Uncle Farid and Aunt Afifa are childless, but as long as I can remember and as often as I have come around, whether announced or unannounced, the two have always sat at their table with guests. Relatives, neighbours, colleagues arrive and all find the table richly set.

Uncle Farid cooks well. In fact his appetisers are really good. Some of our aunts, uncles or friends could prepare this or that particular dish better. But no one can create the abundance of dishes that is a part of Damascus's most famous speciality as well as he does. We are talking of *mezzeh* or *mezze*, or, as some Damascenes with their preference for elongated vowels say, *maaza*. The likely Persian-Arabic origin of the term maaza and exactly what it means are debated to this day. But in Syria and the Lebanon people always take it to be a diverse arrangement of appetizers. It is amazing that Damascenes consider such a huge spread simply as appetite enhancers. That is why it shows up in most Damascene cookbooks and menus as a starter, Arabic *muqabbilat*, rather as in Italy filling spaghetti and antipasti are only considered to be appetisers.

Uncle Farid always prepares everything fresh. He whirls around in his tiny kitchen while his wife carries the decorated plates to the table in the courtyard. Aunt Afifa is a quiet epicure. She delights in her good fortune to have met a man who champs at the bit to start cooking and always sings while doing so – loudly and off key, but with great joy. His accompanying orchestra are the sizzling oil, the hissing meat, the drumming mortar, and the explosion of nuts under his wooden hammer. The aroma of spices and herbs wraps itself around his singing voice like a transparent silk scarf from the Arabian Nights. Aunt Afifa arranges the brimming bowls, platters, large cups and little porcelain boats on the table. She scatters rose petals and jasmine blossoms in between and places glasses next to the plates.

Maaza, the sea of appetizers, is a typical Damascene invention, because there is hardly any other dish better suited for entertaining. At Uncle Farid's, you spend three to five hours at the table. He is so precise in his preparations that he rarely gets up during the meal and then only for water, ice cubes or to replenish a platter. Aunt Afifa is not allowed to move at all. She is always queen of the table and that is what he calls her, too. Some people completely forget her real name is Afifa and call her *Malake*, Queen, instead.

Uncle Farid's secret is that he recognised early on that many components of maaza taste best when eaten warm. So he puts the dishes on little hot plates so his guests can eat at their leisure until late into the night.

My mother, who rarely praised a cook, because she herself was one of the best, made a clear exception with Uncle Farid. 'Many could cook one or other dish better, but every cook in Damascus could take lessons from him on how he composes his maaza.'

And he really does compose. Often he offers ten and not infrequently twenty different dishes. He made a special maaza when his wife, as if by a miracle, survived a heart operation. He waited until she had fully recovered and then invited everyone to what he called a 'celebratory gathering to give thanks for good fortune'.

The guests – and I, with Mother and Father, was lucky to be amongst them – were agape with astonishment. There were 50 dishes on a gigantic table, which was how old Aunt Afifa was that year. The eye has rarely been as spoiled as it was on that late afternoon.

Seven appetisers are an absolute must before you can even begin to use the word maaza. Then you can add as many others as you like. That is why I have put Uncle Farid's seven favourites at the top of his maaza list.

Each of the following listed components of a maaza is a meal in itself and, as we will mention later, there are at least two or three variations of every dish. Clearly, there is plenty of room for your own imagination in a maaza. Maaza can be a few unpretentious little plates of nibbles and it can become a dream table from the Arabian Nights.

Sometimes Uncle Farid constrains himself to only vegetarian appetisers, sometimes he replaces meat with chicken or fish, but he never brings all the different types of meats together, as is the rule in restaurants. He always says you should not mix up the spheres when eating: air, earth or water.

For drinks he serves chilled and diluted Arak, dry wines and juices and the finale, as always with Arabs, is a lovely Arabic mocha with cardamom. Uncle Farid knows that coffee and cardamom not only leave a good taste in the mouth for the return home, but also – and he swears to this – help with the digestion. That was the secret, he said, of the Arabs when they were still living healthily.

The quantities given below are such that each of the dishes of the maaza could serve as a main course. If a dish is to be prepared as part of a larger maaza, then a quarter of these quantities will suffice. Uncle Farid has developed a clever system: dishes that have been finished to the last crumb over a number of maaza evenings move up the list of favourites, while any dish that has barely been touched over several nights is struck from the list altogether.

As guests are meant to serve themselves, it is worth placing each dish on two platters so every guest can reach it. Besides, two smaller full plates are more attractive to the eye than a single large one. The arrangement of the table should be an invitation to reverie. The symphony of colours and plates should tempt you to try every dish.

The host should encourage the guests to pass the plates to each other, which has always proven useful with the large groups that gather around Uncle Farid's table. 'This way the guests lose some of their shyness, which is what any good host wants,' Uncle Farid whispers with a smile.

✳ حمص بطحينة ✳

1. Hummus
Purée of chickpeas and ground sesame paste

500 g dried chickpeas
300 g ground sesame paste (Tahini)
2 lemons
2 garlic cloves
2 tsp salt
2 tbsp cumin
1 bunch parsley
1 tsp paprika
100 ml olive oil
200 g pine nuts

Wash the chickpeas and soak in plenty of water overnight. (They will double in volume.) Then boil for 2 hours. Drain the chickpeas with a sieve, reserving the broth.

Chop up the chickpeas in a food processor. A smooth cream (paste) needs to develop.

Add the tahini (sesame paste, not to be confused with sesame oil), juice of 2 lemons, peeled and crushed garlic cloves, salt and cumin to the chickpea cream. Mix it all together and purée until smooth. If necessary, add a bit of the reserved broth so the porridge really becomes creamy. It must be smooth, but thick, neither becoming soupy nor full of dry lumps. Spread the cream on several flat bowls or plates.

This works best if you put a portion of the paste in the middle of the bowl and use a spoon to spread it out into a 1 cm thick layer and smooth out the edge with a damp finger.

Garnish the surface with chopped parsley, paprika, cumin and *olive oil. Keep in mind that you can make nice designs with the three colours, green (parsley), red (paprika) and yellow (cumin).*

Carefully fry the pine nuts until they are golden brown and sprinkle them over the hummus.

❋ *Boil the chickpeas in the water they have soaked in as this water contains many important minerals. Skim off any foam and keep adding water while cooking if necessary. The water must cover the chickpeas the entire time.*

2. Tabbouleh

(see Page 12)

❋ خضار مقلية ❋

3. Deep Fried or Fried Vegetables

Deep Fried Cauliflower
1 large or 2 small cauliflower heads

Remove stems and leaves from the cauliflowers. Wash the florets and dry. If they are large, halve them with a sharp knife. Then deep-fry them in a neutral oil (sunflower oil is best) until brown. (Do not cook them beforehand!) Keep turning the little florets until they are evenly brown.

Arrange them in a large bowl so the little stems point toward the centre of the bowl, where a small plate of lemon slices can be balanced. Season lightly with salt and pepper just before serving.

❋ *Never use olive oil for frying. It has too intensive a flavour.*

A hint of lemon juice on the cauliflower intensifies its real flavour.

Once you have tasted fried cauliflower, this will be the only way you will ever prepare it in the future.

Deep Fried Aubergines
1 kg fresh, smooth aubergines

Wash the aubergines and remove the stem end. Starting at the top, peel off a strip of skin, then leave some and peel off another strip.

Then cut the aubergine in 1 cm slices, lightly salt and set aside for 10 minutes. Pat the slices dry with a light touch and deep fry in oil.

Keep turning them so the aubergine browns evenly.

Do not add any more salt; just sprinkle a touch of ground pepper over them.

❄ Salt draws the bitterness out of the aubergine and closes the pores so it does not absorb too much oil.

Leave the fried aubergines to drain on kitchen towel for 5 minutes and then serve on a plate. Season with a bit of pepper and sprinkle chopped parsley over them.

Fried Sweet Peppers
1 kg red, green and yellow sweet peppers

Wash the peppers; remove the stem and seeds. Cut the peppers into 2–3 cm thick strips and fry in oil.

Fried Courgettes
1 kg young, small courgettes (zucchini)

Wash the courgettes and remove the ends. Slice in rounds or strips and leave to dry for an hour on kitchen towel. Keep turning them over. The drier they are the better they will taste. Fry only briefly in a bit of oil so they retain their flavour. Drain on kitchen towel. Place in a bowl and drizzle with a bit of olive oil. Season to taste with salt and pepper.

4. Kibbeh

(see Page 26)

5. Falafel

(see Page 43)

٭ سلطة خيار مع لبن ٭

6. Yoghurt with Cucumber, Garlic and Mint

2 cucumbers
1 kg full fat plain yoghurt
2 garlic cloves
1 tsp salt
1 tbsp mint
Peel the cucumbers and cut into small dice. Add to the yoghurt.
Add the crushed garlic, salt and pepper and stir.
Full fat yoghurt is better suited for this than low fat yoghurt.

7. Pasties

(see Page 16)

8. Aubergine Purée with Yoghurt or Lemon

(see Page 113)

٭ صبانغ بالقشطة ٭

9. Spinach with Sour Cream or Yoghurt

1 kg spinach (fresh or frozen)
500 g sour cream, crème fraiche or yoghurt
2 large onions
2 tbsp olive oil
4 garlic cloves

6 walnuts
3 tbsp coriander
1 knife tip cayenne pepper
1 tsp salt
1 lemon

Wash the spinach or defrost if frozen. Squeeze out excess water.
Peel the onions, finely chop and fry to a golden brown in the
olive oil. Add the finely chopped garlic and immediately add
the spinach leaves. Steam for about 10 minutes. Then add 4
walnuts chopped small and the spices. Drizzle the lemon over it
and allow to cool.
After cooling, mix in the sour cream or yoghurt. Spread on a
platter and garnish with the remaining chopped walnuts.
Sour cream gives the dish a substantial feel, while yoghurt
makes it more refreshing.

10. Bread Salad

(see Page 23)

11. Kebab

(see Page 61)

٭ ورق عنب بالزيت ٭

12. Yaprak
Stuffed Vine Leaves with Vegetarian Filling
Only the vegetarian stuffed vine leaves are suitable as a cold
appetizer. Those stuffed with meat taste best when served warm.

Vegetarian Filling
500 g vine leaves
250 g long grain rice

1 bunch flat leaf parsley
2 large onions
2 garlic cloves
150 ml olive oil
2 tbsp dried chickpeas
2 tsp salt
1 tsp coriander
1 tsp paprika
2 tsp mint
½ tsp pepper
1 tsp cinnamon
2 untreated lemons (for cooking)

Put the chickpeas to soak overnight the evening before.

Before preparing the vegetarian filling, peel the chickpeas by squeezing them between the forefinger and thumb. The skin will come off and the chickpea split in half.

Combine the chickpeas, salt and all the spices together with the rice. Peel and finely chop the onions; wash and chop the parsley leaves; add to the rice mixture and stir thoroughly. Peel and crush the garlic, mixing with 100 ml of olive oil and add it all to the rice mixture. Stir thoroughly again.

Fill and cook the vine leaves as described on page 35.

When the vine leaves are done, drizzle 50 ml olive oil over them, cover and let stand 5 minutes. Then serve. Vine leaves with a vegetarian filling can be served cold or hot.

❁ First start with half the filling. Should the wrapping cause a problem, you can also prepare the stuffing separately. Barely cover the rice mixture with water and simmer over a low heat for 20 minutes until the water was been absorbed. Leave to rest for another 5 minutes. Serve with a small salad.

❊ زيت و زعتر ❊

13. Zahtar and olive oil

*You will only find Zahtar at an Arab grocer. The spice mixture
will keep, if well sealed, for up to a year and is very inexpensive.
The best mixture does not come from Damascus, but rather from
Aleppo, Arabic zahtar halabi. Serve the spice mixture in small
bowls with small bowls of olive oil next to it. Dip a piece of bread
in the oil and then lightly press it into the spice mixture. Always
only take a bite-sized piece of bread. Never dunk a piece of bread
with a bite taken out of it in the oil.*

❊ جبنة ❊

14. Cheese

An assortment of cheeses

❊ لبنة ❊

15. Quark
(Low fat soft cheese or Curd)

*Quark is an easy and terrific example of how good even simple
dishes can taste.*

*Mix the quark, with or without garlic, with a pinch of salt and
fresh herbs selected to taste.*

*You can also finely dice a tomato or cucumber and mix it in.
Drizzle with a bit of olive oil.*

Goes well with bread.

❈ *Choose herbs according to preference (parsley, mint,
oregano, thyme and chives are best suited for this) but try not to
use too many different types of herbs.*

Quark is also delicious with dried herbs or spices like cumin.

Only quark with at least 40 to 50 per cent fat content will give you the full flavour.

✻ خس وخضار ✻

16. Fresh Salads

Wash and chop crisp fresh salad leaves (only the young, inner leaves), tomatoes, cucumbers, carrots, sweet peppers. Serve in bowls. They are a pleasure for eyes and palate.

✻ *Several bowls of olives and pickled vegetables, along with pistachios and peanuts, make the table even more colourful. Of course, bread must never be lacking at a maaza and some hosts also make fresh fruit available.*

For lovers of spicier notes in their food, little bowls of ground cumin, sweet paprika, ground allspice, ground pepper, thyme, curry powder (medium hot), whole red or pink pepper corns, salt and cardamom pods for added seasoning distributed around the table also look great.

The farewell or
Of car horns, kisses and church bells

My sister returned home and rang me. I saw her number on the display *and wanted to tease her. 'Wrong number, Ma'am,' I said. She laughed. 'Ringing you and getting a wrong number! That doesn't make sense. I wanted to say good-bye with a symphony of noise from Damascus. I'll keep silent for five minutes. I don't know whether you can describe this, but background noise is one of the most important things in a city.'*

She fell silent.

Damascus is a carpet of noise and sound with many layers. The sound changes from area to area. Whether there is a point in heaven where all these sounds are mixed together, is beyond my knowing. The noises surrounding our house in the Old City are modern, a mixture of car sounds, horns and music, a little muted. Every once in a while these sounds press into the foreground, most often at night and during siesta time, when the quarter is quiet. The car horns especially! Arabs sound their horns not in anger or at moments of danger, but because they enjoy sounding their horns. They take pleasure in musically announcing: 'Hello, it's me! Do you like my car horn?' That is why many make the extra effort to have their horns retrofitted and get something installed that is more musical than the standard issue. They beat on the horn in a rhythmic tattoo so – from a distance – you could almost enjoy it, rather than wishing the great-grandparents of these tooting drivers in hell because they produced this Satan's brood who mug you from behind with their horns.

In the distance you can also hear the voice of Feiruz, the best singer of the Middle East, blended with the voice of the muezzin and the singsong of a street vendor. On the telephone I could not understand what he was selling, but I could hear that he had a good voice. A mother calls to her young daughter because she wants to give her a kiss. I laughed because I had to think of my mother who would also sometimes out of sheer joy call me from the street, hug me and kiss me. I was astounded that she really did not want anything other than to satisfy her yearning for me.

The bells of a church ring out the sounds of mourning. A monotone sequence always heralds a funeral. Children whoosh past our door singing and before the sounds of their confused voices can reach my ear they have already disappeared again.

Marie returned to the telephone with a laugh. 'That is Damascus,' she said. 'I just realised that I still have a lot to tell you. But I have to go now. I'll continue another time. Okay? Until then, be happy.'

I could have listened to her for years.

As I rang off, I recalled the melancholy farewell of the French poet Alphonse de Lamartine as he left my city in 1832:

'We left Damascus and climbed up the mountain to have a last look. We paused to absorb the heavenly view. In that moment I understood why so many locate the lost paradise in Damascus ...'

The best way to enjoy an ancient city

Damascus is no place for the whistle-stop tourist. That said, it's less about the sheer length of time you spend there than the intensity of that time. That's the thing about ancient cities. They only really reveal themselves to those with open hearts and eyes; otherwise, they can camouflage themselves to the point of anonymity.

Better, then, to savour a few parts of the city in depth rather than attempt a lightning tour through 8000 years of history. Here, slowness is synonymous with respect. And Damascus certainly warrants a respectful approach.

The friendliness of the city's inhabitants is renowned worldwide. In fact, some people go so far as to accuse the ancient metropolis' citizens of having too polite and diplomatic a smile ready for every visitor. But that's more envy talking than the considered view of a connoisseur of human nature.

Sure, hospitality can sometimes be cloying and overbearing, but it can also mean something as simple and kind as a drink of water proffered at a hot, dusty spot or a smiling, sympathetic face at a time of sadness. Indeed, a smile is exactly what a nervous, anxious, tired stranger wants to see. The people of Damascus know that and so go out of their way to make visitors feel at home.

There are liars and cheats everywhere, even among those who take a mistrustful and unfriendly attitude toward strangers.

Just as you only truly value good health when you fall ill, you only really notice how much you miss Damascus when you're leaving it. This yearning makes its presence felt shortly after take-off, like some invisible, shy fairy. You glance over your shoulder, feeling a sudden powerful urge to return, but too late – the plane's already lifted off the tarmac. But your sense of longing flies off anyway – illicitly, as it were, without a boarding pass – winging its way back to the city's alleys. And once there, taking a leisurely stroll round the narrow streets and courtyards and dropping in at the cafés and restaurants, it keeps firing off excited little messages to you. It makes you forget the hustle and bustle of Damascus, and the dodgy carpet that you bought, and all the tiresome bureaucrats with their endless official stamps, and you vow to fly back there yourself at the first opportunity and calm your yearning. Only this time, you swear you'll bring the city back with you – but of course that's as impossible as trying to carry water home in a sieve.

How can it be, though, that strangers feel nostalgic for Damascus?

Damascus is one of the oldest continuously occupied cities in the world. By the time the ‚Eternal City' of Rome was built, Damascus had already been in existence for 1000 years, and was the capital of the Aramaeans. It's this continuity that provides the key to the Damascene psyche.

Egyptian, Aramaic, Greek, Babylonian, Persian, Jewish, Roman, and Arab cities and empires arose and flourished, and in their first flush of youthful splendour eclipsed the city of Damascus and subjugated it – before eventually growing moribund and collapsing as a result of wars, plagues or natural disasters. But Damascus remained. In their haste to leave the city, these various cultures left behind a small part of themselves in the alleys of the metropolis. Wandering round them, you might hear a snatch of music from Rome or the odd word from Greece, or catch a waft of African spices, French pastries or even Latin American cooking, brought back by Syrian emigrants and sailors. According to their identity cards, the people of Damascus are Arabs, but all these civilisations that once made their mark on the city have also left indelible traces on the Damascene soul. In sum, Damascus is one huge cultural lost-property office.

So it is, then, that one of the myriad colours among the thousand-and-one mosaic tiles that make up the city of Damascus will suddenly strike a chord in the visitor's heart. This sensation is one of love, and love is the mother of all longing.

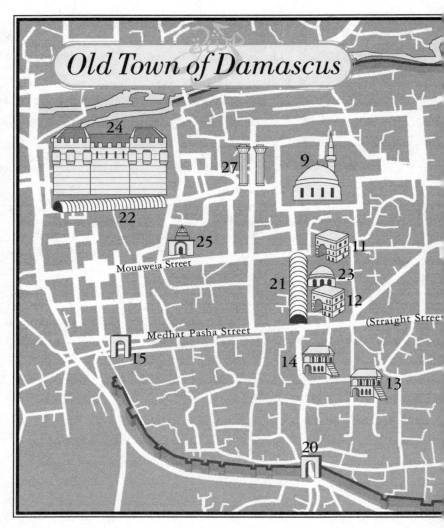

Old Town of Damascus

1 Ananias Chapel
2 Franciscan Monastery
3 Jesuit Church
4 Church of the Maronites

5 Miryamiyya Church
(Greek Orthodox)
6 Church of St George
(Syrian Orthodox)
7 Syrian Catholic Church

8 Bakri Hammam
9 Umayyad Mosque
10 Anbar House
11 Azem Palace
12 Khan al Azem
13 Nizam House

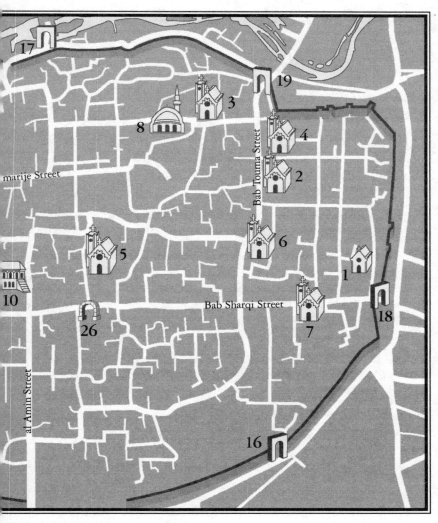

14 as Sibai House	**20** Bab as Saghir	**24** Citadel
15 Bab al Jabiye	**21** Bzouriyya souq	**25** Maristan Nureddin
16 Bab Kisan	(spice market)	**26** Roman arch
17 Bab as Salam	**22** Souq al Hamidiyya	**27** Temple of Jupiter
18 Bab ash Sharqi	**23** Hammam Nureddin	
19 Bab Touma		

The Dark Side of Love

SHORTLISTED FOR *THE INDEPENDENT*
FOREIGN FICTION PRIZE 2010

Murder mystery, epic love story, Rafik Schami's dazzling novel explores a century of Syrian history and politics – but at its heart lie the compelling stories of three generations of lovers who risk death rather than deny their passions.

Damascus, 1967: The body of a high-ranking secret service officer is found hanging in a basket over the city wall above St Paul's Chapel with a mysterious note in his pocket. Frustrated by his country's political corruption, Detective Barudi is determined not to let this case conveniently disappear.

'At last, the Great Arab Novel - appearing without ifs, buts, equivocations, metaphorical camouflage or hidden meanings. Schami's book is exceptional' —*The Independent*

'In The Dark Side of Love, Rafik Schami exploits all the resources of the classic realist novel and then goes a little further... reading the book is always compulsive...The Dark Side of Love illumines almost every side of love, as well as fear, longing, cruelty and lust...A book like this requires a less limiting title. I suggest something as expansive, as comprehensive, as *War and Peace*.' —*The Guardian*

Translated by Anthea Bell
FICTION
£9.99
978-1-906697-24-2

Available Now.

ALSO BY RAFIK SCHAMI

The Calligrapher's Secret

Even as a young man, Hamid Farsi is acclaimed as a master of the art of calligraphy. But as time goes by, he sees that weaknesses in the Arabic language and its script limit its uses in the modern world. In a secret society, he works out schemes for radical reform, never guessing what risks he is running.

His beautiful wife, Nura, is ignorant of the great plans on her husband's mind. She knows only his cold, avaricious side. No wonder she feels flattered by the attentions of his amusing, lively young apprentice. And so begins a passionate love story – the love of a Muslim woman and a Christian man.

Translated by Anthea Bell
FICTION
£17.99, harback
978-1-906697-28-0

Available October 2010